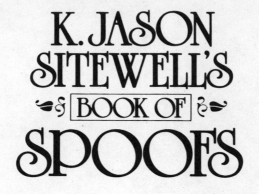

K. JASON SITEWELL'S
BOOK OF
SPOOFS

K. JASON SITEWELL'S

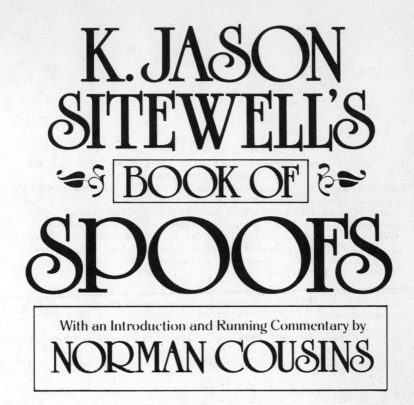

BOOK OF

SPOOFS

With an Introduction and Running Commentary by
NORMAN COUSINS

E. P. DUTTON   NEW YORK

Library of Congress Cataloging-in-Publication Data   Sitewell, K. Jason.
[Book of spoofs]   K. Jason Sitewell's book of spoofs: with an introduction and
running commentary / by Norman Cousins. — 1st ed.   p.   cm.   Selection of
stories published in Saturday review by an anonymous author using the pen
name of K. Jason Sitewell.   ISBN 0-525-24777-7   I. Cousins, Norman.   II.
Title.   III. Title: Book of spoofs.   PN6727.S53B6   1989   814'.54—dc19
88-36421   CIP   Designed by Earl Tidwell   10 9 8 7 6 5 4 3 2 1   First
Edition

Grateful acknowledgment is given for permission to quote excerpts from the
following works:

"The Games Magazines Play" from *The Christian Science Monitor,* by Frederick
Hunter. Reprinted by permission from *The Christian Science Monitor.* Copyright
© 1974 The Christian Science Publishing Society. All rights reserved.

"A Frightening Bill" and "The Conspiracy Against Golf" from the *Richmond
Times-Dispatch,* by Charles McDowell Jr., 1971. Reprinted by permission.

Excerpts from "Golf's Finest Hour" from *The Saturday Evening Post,* by Jim
Bergman. Copyright © 1978 by The Curtis Publishing Co.

"The Greatest Feat in the History of Golf," "The Astounding Story of the
Golfing Gorillas," "How I Taught Golda Meir to Play Golf—Almost," "The
Great Japanese Golf Plot," and "The Worst Played Hole in the History of Golf"
from *Golf Digest.* Copyright © 1988. Reprinted by permission of *Golf Digest.*

"The Sad Saga of Charlie and Wilma" from *The Miami News,* by John Keasler,
1975. Reprinted by permission.

To Cleveland Amory, André Baruch, Dev Freeman,
Sy Gomberg, and Joel Hammil, who have inexplicably
and nobly survived their relationship with K.J.S.

Contents

vii

Acknowledgments

First of all, my thanks to the readers of the *Saturday Review* for encouraging K. Jason Sitewell over the years and indulging his forays. My thanks to the staff of *SR* for cleaning up the office and restoring order after K.J.S.'s too frequent visits. Appropriate thanks to the writers of letters to the editor of *SR*, participating in the various outrages begun by K.J.S.

Next, Jean Anderson is to be thanked for bringing together Mr. Sitewell's contributions to the *Saturday Review* and *Golf Digest,* both of which have generously given permission to publish the articles by K.J.S. appearing in their pages.

Finally, copious thanks to Mrs. Sitewell, whose ability to put up with K.J.S.'s caprices over many years transcends all understanding.

Introduction

For at least twenty years, during my editorship of the *Saturday Review,* an improbable character by the name of K. Jason Sitewell stalked its pages. Most of his contributions appeared during the first week of April each year, leading many readers to sniff suspiciously at some of the bizarre notions that appeared over his name. Frequently capricious but never malicious, he would give rise to oddities, such as the article on the man who invented the punctuation mark represented by the dot at the end of this sentence. He was responsible almost single-handedly for the public campaign against a bill introduced in the Congress that would have had the effect of abolishing golf. K. Jason Sitewell, it can now be told, was also the author of many of the outrageous notices that appeared in the "Personals" columns of the classified advertising section of the *Saturday Review*.

The attempt to unmask K. Jason Sitewell was notoriously unsuccessful for many years until one of the members of *SR*'s staff, doodling over his name, discovered that it was an imperfect anagram for "Well, it's a joke, son." One would think that Sitewell, thus exposed, would give up his capers and return to his private enterprises, whatever they were. But no; the disclosure had exactly the opposite effect. The intensity and range of his crusades deepened. He wrote, for example, about the origin of the bagel, leading to one of the most voluminous outpourings from readers in the history of the magazine. He probed into anthropology and presented the sad finding that Darwin had been looking through the wrong end of the telescope; the evidence he amassed showed that the apes were descended from man. He presented the genealogical evidence that George Washington had Russian ancestors. He carried on a relentless war against the computerization of daily existence.

In short, Sitewell was a spoofer. He was not merely tolerated but actually encouraged by the editor. Why? The answer, if an answer is needed, is that life is serious but it need not be solemn. Spoofs and hoaxes help to remove some of the starchiness that makes everyday existence a lot stiffer than it ought to be. They help to take the stuffing out of shirts, whoever and wherever the wearers may be. They also lead us to lie down in green pastures and to experience a restoration of souls.

The *Saturday Review* was a journal of ideas and the arts. It was heavily involved in the leading issues of its time, but beyond all its concerns and causes was a deep belief in the enjoyment of living and a delight in the gift of hearty laughter. The pages of the magazine featured articles from some of the leading thinkers of the period—Lewis Mumford, John Dewey, H. G. Wells, Arthur Koestler, Harold Nicolson, Irwin Edman among them—but these articles were also interspersed with humorous cartoons, which the editor insisted on selecting himself. Art directors of magazines tend to resent cartoons because they use up space that would otherwise go to artwork or photographs. But the cartoons prevailed—to the greater gain, I trust, of the readers.

K. Jason Sitewell wasn't the only source of innocent merriment in the *Saturday Review*. But he became something of a symbol of the magazine's efforts to offset the tensions of modern life even as it sought to cope with them.

A word about spoofing: A spoof and a practical joke are not the same—not by far. Practical jokes can be mean, even vicious. By contrast, everyone can enjoy a spoof. No pie is on anyone's face; no chair is pulled back to send someone sprawling. The very fact that a spoof usually involves a group rather than an individual takes the sting out for any single person. Also, a spoof generally has a point to make, as in Sitewell's spoof about the bill in Congress to outlaw golf. The golf spoof came in the middle of the Vietnam War when many of the country's young people were caught up in protests. They were heavily criticized by some of their older fellow citizens for not recognizing that government, acting on the basis of superior knowledge, was confronted with the need to make responsible decisions. What the golf hoax did was to demonstrate that everyone has a flashpoint for protest, including those who tended to think there is something untidy and irreverent about raising one's voice against officialdom.

In any event, this book brings together the major spoofs appearing over the name of K. Jason Sitewell. Neither the staff members during my tenure at the *Saturday Review,* nor my successors, are to be taxed with responsibility for their origins or their effects. Anyone engaging in calculated nonsense, even as a counterbalance to an oppressive gravity, cannot expect to find safety in numbers.

N.C.

NOTE: The reason for the variations in the name of the magazine is that it began as *The Saturday Review of Literature* and went through successive changes as *The Saturday Review, Saturday Review,* and *Saturday Review/World.*

K. JASON SITEWELL'S
BOOK OF
SPOOFS

All Hail
the Bagel

Just when the bagel entered the American consciousness
it is difficult to say. Certainly it was an ethnic product and
was in favor for many years among those whose families
had their origins in Eastern Europe. But it was not as
familiar, say, as the hot dog until perhaps the middle of
the twentieth century. In any case, Horace Sutton wrote
about the bagel in the *Saturday Review* in the issue of
November 21, 1964.

Sutton is a story by himself. Redheaded and freckled

and looking as though he had just been created by Mark Twain, he came to the office of the magazine in his early twenties and proposed a regular travel column. At that time, we were still called *The Saturday Review of Literature.* How would a travel department fit into a predominantly literary journal? Horace supplied the rationale. The column would be called "Booked for Travel" and would be tailored to meet the needs of thoughtful travelers who might be less interested in the Piccadilly Circus than the British Museum. He presented us with a portfolio of his writings. Like the man himself, his articles were full of zest, high style, and intellectual curiosity.

Thus began one of the most popular features in the history of the magazine. We quickly came to realize that Horace Sutton was much more than a travel writer; he was one of the most versatile and talented journalists of his time. His articles on major world events and his investigative reporting at home and abroad played an important part in the magazine's rapid growth during the fifties and sixties. Horace also had a highly developed sense of fun, which endeared him to the readers all the more. His columns were unpredictable and embraced a wide range of subjects, all the way from famous bistros to the secret of the bagels. One of his articles traced the origin of the bagel to the invasion of Vienna by Turkey in 1683. The Turks left behind crescent-shaped rolls that came to be known as *buegels.* Horace's research produced the information that Austrian Jews who migrated to Galicia brought the *buegels,* or bagels, with them. We weren't prepared for the fact that bagel scholars abounded among our subscribers. For more than two months the magazine was the beneficiary of voluminous research from readers on the origin of the bagel. Who could have suspected that this hardened little object would engage the systematic thought of some of America's finest minds? We had no choice but to reflect these preoccupations on the letters page opposite the editorial. Incidentally, we suspected that K.J.S. used several pen names in his communications to the magazine in order to accommodate the vast store of original information he had accumulated on the subject.

Letters to the Editor

BATTLE OF THE BAGELS

Sir:

Horace Sutton's historical informants at El Al, who associate the introduction of coffee and bagels to Vienna with the Turkish siege of 1683 [*SR*, November 21], are repeating a story that is—to use local idiom—pure *Schmoarr'n* (i.e., a flour and sugar omelet dessert). Coffee is documented in the Austrian capital as early as 1663. Kolschitzky, the alleged "Pole," was probably a Rascian, a Banat Serb, and he surely did not open the first coffeehouse, an institution that dates from a later time than the immediate post-siege period. He was merely one of the city's first *Kaffeesieder* or dispensers, an official privilege granted him as a reward for his heavily self-publicized services as a secret courier during Vienna's ordeal. At this time, moreover, there were few, if any, Jews around, a major expulsion having taken place a decade before the Ottoman attack. In short, the tale is the Austrian and perhaps also the Yiddish equivalent of George Washington and the cherry tree.

Thomas M. Barker
Professor of History
State University of New York
Albany, N.Y.

ह৯

Sir:

Horace Sutton's article about bagels [*SR,* November 21] is excellent. I am sure he will be pleased to learn the true facts concerning the discovery of the bagel:

In 381 B.C., in Crete, there lived a baker named Bagelus. Now, Bagelus had gout. At that time, the standard remedy for gout (cf. Hippocrates) was to encase the large toe in warm dough. One day Bagelus was basking in the hot sun, his feet propped up, in order to give his dough-ringed toes the full benefit of the heat. It was an unusually hot day in Crete. In fact, Cleides tells us (*Heat and Humidity in Ancient Athens,* Olympian Press, 1864) that the temperature on that particular day reached 117 degrees. The dough on Bagelus's toes hardened. When he awakened, he discovered on his toes a fully formed and hardened formation of large brown rings. He also discovered that all the animals in the neighborhood, attracted by the odor, were now pressing in upon him, trying to eat the rings off his feet. Bagelus removed the baked ringlet from his left foot, sniffed at it, then bit into it, experiencing a most delectable and irresistible taste sensation.

It is not known whether Bagelus thereafter hired men to sit in the sun with baked dough ringed around their toes in order to get the authentic sun-baked confection, or whether he synthesized the product in his own bakeshop.

Be that as it may, ancient Greece was introduced to the Bagelus ring, later known as the bagel.

It is true that the bagel has been appreciated and developed mainly in Jewish cooking; but now that the bagel is becoming universalized, it may be well to set the matter straight concerning its historical origin in ancient Greece.

K. Jason Sitewell

ह&

Sir:

The Lowly Bagel, how it has risen! Practically half a Sutton article [*SR,* November 21] devoted to it, which, in turn, elicits letters to the editor! Perforce I must add my comments.

The origins of that threat-to-all-dentures morsel, the bagel, are unimportant. What is intriguing is the interest the hard roll engenders in enthusiast and uninitiated alike. In 1948, when I was a fledgling writer on Madison Avenue, a friend came up with a bagel idea. For 65 cents he would deliver to your door every Sunday morning a packet containing lox, bagels, and cream cheese (traditional Sunday breakfast for many families in Jewish neighborhoods of New York). His deliveries were made anywhere in the city by a crew of disabled World War II veterans.

Enthralled with the idea, I took it to Clementine Paddleford, who blessed the enterprise with a glowing article in the *Herald Tribune.* The result: thousands of telephone calls clamoring for delivery.

Further, a full-page picture in the now-defunct magazine *Pic* showed my friends, on a Sunday morning, pouring cascades of fresh bagels onto assembly tables prior to filling orders. That picture triggered the memory of a rabbi in Puerto Rico who wired us to send the delicacy Air Express.

All of which proves that bagel aficionados go to rare lengths to obtain that tidbit referred to by *SR* as a cement-like roll.

Lillian Pierson Cohen
Gloversville, N.Y.

ह‍ॐ

Sir:

After reading Professor Sitewell's letter on the origin of the bagel [*SR,* December 26] I feel compelled to bring certain additional facts to the attention of your readers. While the Bagelus theory once had wide acceptance, it has now fallen into disrepute. In fact, among students of the area it is generally known as the "Bagelus Fallacy."

While the incident described by K. Jason Sitewell no doubt occurred, since it is referred to by both Tacitus and Livy, it was not the bagel that Bagelus discovered but the doughnut.

Recent translations of latterly discovered Dead Sea Scrolls prove conclusively that the bagel was eaten by the Essenes as early as 527 B.C. and probably considerably before that date. In those days it was known as the *legab*. Undoubtedly, the corruption occurred upon its introduction to modern languages, which, as you know, are written in the opposite direction from ancient Hebrew, or, as we scholars say, backwards.

It is generally believed that the *legab* or bagel was introduced to Crete by one of the ships belonging to the fleet sponsored jointly by King Solomon and the king of

6

Phoenicia. It was an immediate success and it was only after Bagelus discovered the doughnut that its popularity as a breakfast food was somewhat diminished. This in part was due to the fact that the bagel was at this time made in the form of a square. It was only much later that the Greek mathematician Archimedes, while attempting to find the most perfect natural form, suggested that the bagel should be made round.

Even today there remains a hard core of bagel devotees who claim that the full succulence of the bagel can be savored only when it is in the shape of a square. In fact, there exists in Israel today a bagel company that manufactures bagels only in the traditional shape. The famous singing commercial "A Kauffman Square Bagel can't roll off your table" is well known throughout the Middle East.

Mendel Trubnick
Algernon Professor of
    Semitic Semantics
Queens College
Flushing, N.Y.

ح

Sir:

Professor Sitewell's letter on the origin of the bagel in ancient Greece missed by a wide margin. It is true that Bagelus, a Greek, covered his toes with dough in accordance with the accepted remedy for gout at the time. It is also true that the doughy rings hardened one day while Bagelus was baking his gouty feet in the sun. But, unbeknownst to Bagelus and, apparently, to Mr. Sitewell, a hardened dough ring had been discovered in ancient Egypt at least one thousand years earlier. The account is

7

to be found in Fuller's *History of Ancient Egypt.* I quote:

"In 1382 B.C. a superstition seized the people of Alexandria. Suddenly and inexplicably, the notion took hold that demons were inhabiting mummified corpses, causing the bodies to emerge from their shrouded wrappings at night, placing hexes on the populace. People flocked to the high priests, demanding that the demon be exorcised. The priests announced that the demons could be exorcised only by unwrapping twelve mummies that were at least one thousand years old and dipping the bodies in hot oil."

Fuller says that as each casket was opened, out came not just the mummy but all the favorite possessions of the deceased, which, according to custom, had been placed in the burial box. In some cases, the possessions were rather farfetched. For example, into the casket of Bhagelramesis, a member of the High Court known for his gluttony, had been placed various delicacies such as cakes, fried oysters, and sweetbreads. When Bhagelramesis's box was opened, as might be expected, all the foods had long been completely decomposed—all, that is, except one. Bhagelramesis loved unsweetened doughnuts. For some reason having to do perhaps with the cooking oil used, the doughnuts interred with Bhagelramesis not only had not decomposed, but had become petrified. Further, when Bhagelramesis's mummy and his possessions were soaked in the boiling oil for the purpose of exorcising the demon, the mummy was virtually dissolved but the doughnut came through the ordeal undamaged.

It was inevitable, of course, that one of the witnesses to this ritual should have been both curious and hungry. In this way, history came upon the true discovery of the bagel, or more precisely, the *bhagel,* named after Bhagelramesis. And this no doubt also accounts for the attempt of modern bagel bakers to come as close as possible to the original state of petrification in making their bhagels.

Cull Pepper
University of Alexandria
Alexandria, Egypt

ॐ

Sir:

In attributing the discovery of bagels to Bagelus of ancient Greece, Sitewell overlooks the fact that the Greek climate lacks sufficient heat to produce the adamantine hardness of the bagel. It took the Negev desert, and nothing less, to do this.

The true development of the bagel is related in the Bible, I Samuel 25:18 et seq., where David's amatory excursions are discussed. It is there stated, in part: "Then Abigail made haste, and took two hundred loaves . . . and laid them on asses." Obviously, during the ride through the desert on the bony and lumpy backs of asses, the loaves assumed their now well-known shape and consistency. It needs no imagination to recognize the perversion of her name as well as her character. "Abigail" became "Bigail," which was quickly corrupted to "bagel."

The unfair attempt (bordering, I submit, on anti-Semitism) to deprive us Jews of the credit for this ancient gastronomic horror must be nipped in the bud. Sitewell should check his rumors before rushing into print.

Thomas L. Parsonnet
Newark, N.J.

ॐ

9

Sir:

May I once and for all settle the dispute concerning the origin of the bagel? All that is necessary is to refer to Democritus's account of meteoric findings in ancient Greece, circa the fourth century B.C.

Democritus tells us of the examination of small meteoric specimens by Brasidas of Mitylene. Among these specimens was a piece somewhat in the shape of a doughnut. Brasidas presented this rock to his baker as a gentle means of chiding him for the hardness of his breads. The baker got back at Brasidas by producing an unsweetened doughnut that compared very favorably with the tiny meteorite in impenetrability. Brasidas surprised the baker by taking to the improvisation at once and by ordering several dozen more. Brasidas found that the "meteoric doughnut" (the name for which in Greek is *bah-gral*) became palatable and indeed delectable after soaking for three days in hot olive oil.

The reason modern bagels taste like meteorites is that bakers try to cut corners by soaking the bagels for only a few hours.

George Connors
Professor of Ancient
History
Stanford University
Stanford, Calif.

ॐ

Sir:

I have been retained by my client, George F. Bagel, to seek redress from *Saturday Review* in connection with your article and subsequent letters on the origin of the bagel. Contrary to Mr. Sutton, Professor Pepper, Professor Connors, Professor Trubnick, and Mr. Sitewell, the bagel was not invented or discovered by:

    a) Bagelus of ancient Greece;
    b) Bhagelramesis of ancient Egypt;
    c) Abigail in biblical lore;
    d) Brasidas of ancient Mitylene.

The bagel was invented by Zhelleck P. Bagel in 1893 in New York. It was put on sale for the first time in the Rivington Street Bakery on or about February 10, 1893. A copyright on the word "bagel" was granted to Z. P. Bagel in March 1894.

My client, George F. Bagel, great-grandson of Z. P. Bagel, has asked me to obtain from you suitable retractions and acknowledgments. Because of his respect for *Saturday Review* he would prefer not to sue you for damages, but he feels he is entitled to a public apology and retraction.

James N. Dawson
Dawson and Davidson,
Attorneys
New York, N.Y.

EDITOR'S NOTE: All respect and honor to Mr. G. F. Bagel, but the editors will stand their ground. So far as we know, a lawsuit on the origin of the bagel has never occurred before. It is something of a privilege to be involved in a new experience in human history. We can hardly wait.

৯৩

Sir:

    K. Jason Sitewell and other writers of letters to the editors have shown impressive scholarship where bagels are concerned, yet all have lacked the perseverance to trace the cult of bagelology to its source, the Orient. A study of the Tao Te Ching, by Lao-tzu, abolishes all doubt in the matter.

Consider the title Tao Te Ching, which is translated by R. B. Blakney as *The Book of the Way and Its Virtue*. "Way" is an erroneous translation of the Chinese word *wao-fu*, or "wafer," obviously referring to the bagel, which was accepted by the ancient Chinese as a symbol representing the core of their philosophy.

Consider the following quotation:

Once grasp the great form without form,
And you roam where you will
With no evil to fear,
Calm, peaceful, at ease.

At music and viands
The wayfarer [wafer eater] stops.
But the Way [wafer], when declared,
Seems thin and so flavorless

It is nothing to look at
And nothing to hear;
But used, it will prove
Inexhaustible.

The hole in the bagel was seen as in aesthetic contrast to the encircling dough. Witness:

So advantage is had
From whatever is there;
But usefulness rises
From whatever is not.

These are but a few of the repeated references to the bagel in Chinese literature.

In closing, let me mention briefly that the first Chinese currency was made out of small bagels. The Chinese, when biting the bagel coins to test authenticity, discovered that they were edible. Thus was launched the concept of the bagel as a food.

Susan Sax
Chicago, Ill.

ॐ

Sir:

Let me give you our institute's latest findings on the history and/or origin of the bagel.

Mr. Sutton, Professor Connors, Professor Trubnick, Mr. Sitewell, and the law firm of Dawson and Davidson are all correct as far as they go, but they do not go far enough.

May I refer them to the scholarly text *Essen und Fressen,* by Professors Alter Zeitgeist and H. Besser Kuchenmeister (1886), and especially to chapter 17, entitled "The Bagel: Friend or Foe?"

According to this erudite book, the bagel was accidentally invented by the Neanderthal cave man as a weapon of defense. The cementlike object was hurled at the enemy by an atlatl. It did not kill the enemy, it stunned him; and if it did not stun him, then its delicious aroma so intrigued the adversary that he had to sample it on the spot, thereby making capture inevitable. Among the Neanderthals, the bagel was called "the pacifer," and it is generally believed that its ability to prevent bloodshed and war is the

13

main reason for the bagel's continuous international success.

Whether boon or bane, that "hard, unyielding roll with the hole in the middle" is here to stay, and the energetic correspondence that it has inspired has undoubtedly put smiles of economic contentment on the bagel bakers of the world.

> Guy de Vry
> President
> Independent Institute of
>   Bagel Research
> Malibu, Calif.

ಜೆ

Sir:

In connection with *SR* readers' preoccupation with the bagel, would it interest any of them to learn that my life was once saved by a bagel?

It happened in the Korean War. My dear sweet mother had sent me a box of goodies, prominent among which were six bagels. I stuffed them into various pockets of my overcoat. Our company was stationed about forty miles out of Taegu. We were given the assignment of wiping an enemy guerrilla operation five miles north of our position. I led a detachment of about thirty men. In the course of our maneuvers, we ran into enemy machine-gun activity. I was hit in three places. Miraculously, each place was protected by a bagel and my life was saved. The doctors said that only the adamantine hardness of the bagel could have resisted the force of the bullets.

When, therefore, people speak of the bagel, I get a lump in my throat—and not merely in anticipation of trying to get it down. Surely your readers can report similarly significant accounts of the utility of the bagel.

Bailey Richards
Chicago, Ill.

୫◕

Sir:

Reader Bailey Richards has brought to mind my most vital experience, which would seem incredible except to Bagel Simpaticos.

When I was very young, my Mother gave me a bullet, and she bade me carry it in a breast pocket at all times. This I did, never realizing the Why, but only out of reverence and respect for the Dear Lady.

Many years thereafter, I was in a strange City, and arrived to find myself in the midst of a Bakery Shop price war. This one was so very bitter that the bakers attacked each other with anything they could find. They had on hand a large quantity of bagels, which, even when fresh, are hard enough; these were stale, and the merest stripling knows that the stale bagel is more lethal than a hand-held atomic bomb which has been detonated (Ordnance technicians refer to this weapon as the Stagel: a stale bagel).

I was caught in the cross fire of thrown bagels. I was struck by one in the chest. If not for that bullet, that bagel would have gone right through my heart.

George E. Branch
New Rochelle, N.Y.

୫◕

Sir:

Misconceptions about the origins of the bagel are the inevitable result of the multitude of cultures it has invaded. My own area of expertise is Egyptology. The North African bagel myth has its roots in territories adjacent to the headwaters of the Nile, the habitat of the now-extinct bakelbird, later softened to bagelbird or water bagel. The bakel when frightened would hide its head in its anus, a curious reflex which appears to have been the main cause of the extinction of the species—by suffocation. Many clay models of the bagelbird have been found as far south as Tanganyika, all in the familiar position of the fright reflex. It has been noted that because children of the headwater tribes would often try to eat the clay reproductions, some wise old women started making bagelbird sculptures out of mashed food fibers. *Bakala,* incidentally, was the native expression for "grunt" or "groan," derived from the fact that the bagelbird laid eggs of astonishing size. The groaning sound that it made when laying those enormous eggs has been most accurately described by tribal descendants as "OYYY GEVALT!"

Devery Freeman
Los Angeles, Calif.

॰॰

Sir:

The current buildup in the bagel controversy is clearly an attempt by Israel to obscure her real aim: to place a bagel in orbit around the earth. This is part of a larger campaign to encourage the use of bagels as food for space travelers, as they are already on El Al Airlines.

This information is being dispatched immediately via

Aer Lingus to Shannon and Dublin Castle, with a plea for a crash program to get a shillelagh into orbit before the bagel goes up.

William B. Gallagher, M.D.
La Crosse, Wis.

ह॰

Sir:

With all due respect to Messrs. Sutton, Sitewell, Connors, et al., the bagel was a symbolic representation long before it became a gastronomical indecency. The Bagel Curse, referred to fleetingly in the *Rig Veda,* has recently been identified (from fragments of the *Touli Sap Scroll*) by Professor Lheel of the University Vhee in Cambodia as: "A lox upon thee." During the Khmer era the letter *L* gradually disappeared from the language to be replaced by *P* because of the influx of tribes from the north. This transition period is well documented in what are now known as the LP records.

Interestingly enough, the Khmer word for bagel was *id,* which, in Khmer, was a mother symbol. Dr. Lheel surmises that a disturbed Khmer son, revolted, perhaps, by the compulsion of returning to his mother's womb, constructed an id symbol from Khmer dough in the form of a ring. A ring, by the way, is a representation of what is, in psychoanalytical parlance, the maternal nimbus.

This evolution (and degradation) of the Bagel Legend from Vedic deity (Bagel), to curse, to physical incarnation of id in dough or, more correctly, dough in id, may be the underlying theme of *Tiny Alice.* There is no doubt that Julian (and Dr. Lheel concurs unreservedly in this)

17

personifies the Bagel Legend from its auspicious beginning as a God figure to its ignominious end as a tired tire.

William B. Wright
La Jolla, Calif.

ॐ

Dear Mister:

I am a man ninety-three years old and I get ag-
gravated every time I hear that somebody I never heard
of invented the bagel. Lies like this you don't need when
you reach my age. At ninety-three you got more important
things to worry about. Like, are you going to be alive or
dead when you wake up in the morning. So for the last
time I am going to tell the world who really invented the
bagel. If it's not 100 percent truth may God strike me dead
where I am standing. I mean it and in case He needs new
glasses too I will even say where I'm standing. It is in room
22G and He can't miss it because outside on the window
is still a sticker from the Brooklyn Dodgers. This shows
you how often they clean in this place. But you think my
children believe this? When they have to dig to find me in
the dust like King Tut maybe then they'll believe it. But
why should I aggravate you too with my children? I am
sure your own children give you this kind of pleasure.
Now it is time for the 100 percent truth about who invented the bagel. So I'll tell you once and for all. Straight
from the shoulder.

The bagel was invented by my Uncle Morris. It happened like this. When he was young he made kaiser rolls
in a bakery. But he also wanted to be the life of the party
so he could meet girls. Only there was a problem with this.
He had a small head and a long nose. So when there was

a party and he put on even a medium lampshade to be funny his small head disappeared under it and nobody noticed he was even there. So he decided to make something to fit in case he wasn't invited no place for a while it wouldn't get moldy. But irregardless that's exactly how the bagel got invented. How do I know? Because I was six years old and saw it myself at my Aunt Sophie's party for her son Arnold's bar mitzvah. It was the first time in history anybody ever wore a bagel on his nose and that person was my Uncle Morris and nobody else.

One more thing you should know. How it became something good to eat was because of a girl at the party named Yetta. She weighed like maybe 200 pounds and was Yetta the Fresser. She was called this because she would eat anything that didn't move. So when my Uncle Morris drank too much wine and couldn't move she bit the bagel and fell in love with both of them. It was fine for bagels but not for him. At their wedding she tried to bite his bagel while they were dancing. I will only tell you this. After that he couldn't even wear a cookie on his nose.

Now. There is one more final thing I want to say. If anybody should tell you somebody else invented the bagel just ask them how it got its name if it didn't come from our family? Then tell them to leave me alone.

Harry Bagel
Los Angeles, Calif.

ॐ

Sir:

Research on the bagel has been somewhat complicated and confusing. We do know that it gets its name from the Yiddish word *beigen,* meaning "to bend or twist."

There is a legend that bagels were first made in the form of stirrups in Vienna in 1683—bagel or *buegel* being German for "stirrup." The bakers chose that form to show their gratitude to the king of Poland who liberated them, in commemoration of the fact that many of those liberated clung to the stirrups as the king rode through their town on horseback.

Several years ago, the Israeli government set up a commission to find out who really invented the bagel. That austere body chose one of its most eminent researchers to do just that, funding him with $150,000 over a period of two years. Shlomo Tellig accepted the challenge with high hopes for success and took off on his mission.

Two years later, on schedule, he returned to Israel and reported to the Commission on Bagel Research. The chairman, a distinguished member of the Israeli parliament, greeted him warmly and said:

"Welcome home Shlomo. We hope you had a good trip."

"Indeed I did," said the researcher.

"You have spent two years away from us and $150,000. Have you found out who invented the bagel?"

"Yes," replied Shlomo.

"And?"

"His name was Eddie!"

A. Baruch
Los Angeles, Calif.

ॐ

Sir:

I cannot understand why no mention has been made of the two really authoritative sources on the bagel. These volumes are classics and can be found in any good library.

The earlier one covers the *hegel* (as it was originally called) from its invention by the eminent philosopher one day when he got tired of thinking, right through the long bitter power struggle that followed his death the next week.

German intellectuals of the 1800s, heavy thinkers and heavy eaters, were delighted with their new treat, but a sizable group balked at the name, wishing to memorialize another philosopher, Heinrich Bagel, who had recently been the rage.

Five years and many manifestos later, the "bagelists" emerged triumphant.

In his epic, Karl Marx recorded the above for its future historical interest. He himself considered such values surplus. The bagel was viewed basically. With that sixth sense genius possesses, he foresaw the influence this doughty doughy circle could wield, accurately predicting its use as a reactionary tool against the workers and peasants.

Who, reading his magnificent indictment, *Das Establishment,* can ever forget the opening line, "A specter is haunting Europe, the specter of bagelism"?

It remained for the Russian secret police to fulfill Marx's prophecy in 1905 by bringing in the bagels, thousands upon thousands of them, from Germany to their own country. These provocateurs, whose job it was to stir up and then mow down people susceptible to revolutionary ideas, would mingle with the masses bearing bags full of bagels and urge them to storm the czar's Winter Palace.

Craftily they dropped hints that at the then temperatures (around 55 degrees below zero) bagels made excellent weapons, being harder than rocks though lighter in weight, and thus portable in greater quantities.

Upon hearing this (from counterpolice spies infiltrating the police spies), Vladimir Ilyitch Lenin sat down and wrote the second great treatise on the subject. Its title: *On the Efficacy and Utility of Certain Circular Objects in Effecting a Successful Conclusion of the Class Struggle*, popularly known as "Lenin on the Bagel Question."

The fact that he never referred directly to the provocateurs has two possible interpretations. Either he did not want to get the poor fellows fired, swelling the already swollen unemployed ranks, or they had relatives in the book business.

Be that as it may, he pointed out in 683 dialectically materialistic pages how wrong the suggested approach was.

Yes (or *"Da,"* as he put it), attacking the Winter Palace with bagels might break windows and batter doors but, in the last analysis as well as the fifth and the fifteenth, were these the proper instruments to seize the means of production? *Nyet!* (roughly translated: No!) For this guns were needed. And the ones with guns were the *pascudnyaki* (sons-of-guns) guarding the Winter Palace.

Well, the Bagel Revolution of 1905 took place anyhow. Those who read Lenin's book took his advice and didn't go. But a lot went and got mowed down. These were the ones who couldn't read.

Isn't there a lesson in this for all of us?
　　　　　　　　　　　　Edna Toney
　　　　　　　　　　　　Katonah, N.Y.

୬

Sir:

The bagel was probably the first flying saucer. I have uncovered evidence showing that the bagel was involved in the earliest visitation to the earth from outer space. Professor Carl Heinz von Shtupp of the Koenigsburg Institute of Extraterrestrial Research has discovered mysterious markings on Ecuadorean plateaus as photographed by satellite. Those markings, he believes, are prehistoric landing fields for tiny spacecraft in the shape of the modern bagel. If it should appear that UFOs in the size of bagels were improbable because of the scale, we need to be reminded that everything was a lot smaller in those days. Remains of skeletons show that horses were the size of dogs, and men, if not the size of mice, were no taller than fire hydrants, which, by a curious coincidence, were also the invention of Bagelus, referred to by Mr. Sitewell in his letter.

The term *flying saucers* is only approximate. In truth, they are flying bagels, but the U.F.O. aficionados are reluctant to give it a Jewish spin since they justifiably feel they have trouble enough with credibility.

The cave drawings of Lascaux give substance to Professor von Shtupp's theory. It is clearly noted that between the drawn figures of bison and antelopes there are two men in mortal combat with a woman standing nearby awaiting the outcome. The professor points out a hitherto unnoticed feature that what the woman holds in her left hand is unmistakably a bagel; and it's his point that the men are not fighting over the woman but for possession of the bagel.

The secret of the bagel's origin lies deep in our subconscious, but added proof of the above thesis lies in a simple fact. Who has not—when offered a bagel, embellished with a heavy coating of pellucid cream cheese, on top of which lie choice cuts of lox with perhaps a slice of tomato and onion—who has not exclaimed through his coursing salivary juices, "Out of this world!"

Joel Hammil
Los Angeles, Calif.

THE BAGEL AND PHILOSOPHY

Sir:

> Have a tart,
> Said René Descartes.
>
> No, eat a bagel,
> Urged Friedrich Hegel.
>
> Not without lox!
> Thundered Karl Mox.

Ben Hellman
New York, N.Y.

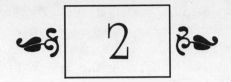

2

Games Magazines Play

One of the favorite sections of the *Saturday Review,* according to the readers' preference polls we took occasionally, was the Classified Department, especially that portion called "Personals." It all began in the early days of the magazine when Louis Untermeyer, the poet and anthologist, wanted to find a buyer for a pet donkey, and wrote a short but touching description of the ass, resulting in a new home for the animal. Christopher Morley, one of *SR*'s founding editors and a talented American essayist noted for his sagacious merriment, was persuaded by the business department to concoct some notices that might add to the reader traffic in the classified pages, thus enhancing the appeal of the section for advertising.

In this way, the back pages of the magazine became a prime reading feature. Regular readers, of course, were readily able to identify the homegrown notices, but occasionally those would serve as the basis for news stories. Once, for example, there appeared this notice:

> WE ARE RECALLING copies of our manual *Build Your Own Dirigible* because of an unfortunate typographical error on p. 67. The sentence which now reads "keep the helium level above .72 at all times" mistakenly has the decimal point before instead of after the 7. We regret any inconvenience. Build Your Own Dirigible Company, Lakehurst, N.J.

One of the New York newspapers picked up the story, first inquiring whether anyone had been hurt.

What the classified section enabled us to do, of course, was to have an outlet for our private piques. We recognized that no one was better qualified to concoct "Personals" notices than K. Jason Sitewell. He couldn't have been more cooperative.

Perhaps the best way of presenting the story of *SR*'s

"Personals" column would be to reprint these excerpts from an article in the *Christian Science Monitor*.

Christian Science Monitor

THE GAMES MAGAZINES PLAY

Readers of *Saturday Review/World* cherish the magazine's classified section where they savor such ads as that for "amusing fictitious degrees." But lately some items have taken on an even more offbeat flavor.

For example, one recent "personal" asked:

> Are you embarrassed to let your dog or cat see the label on the cheap brand of pet food you are feeding him? Our colorful stick-on labels with actual photos of steaks, chicken, and lobster can be easily placed over the labels of the cans you buy. Write to Miss Leading Labels at Camouflage, Inc. SR/W Box PT.

Or how about this dandy item?

> Surprise your tennis partners with helium-filled tennis balls. Guaranteed to disappear from sight on the slightest contact with racquet. Orbit Balls, SR/W Box SL.

"Darned if we didn't get some orders for those dog food labels," says editor Norman Cousins. "And, believe it or not, well-known people wrote in asking about the tennis balls."

"We enjoy a good laugh," Mr. Cousins explains, "and like to share it with our readers. The editors deal with serious things, but that doesn't mean we have to be somber. Laughter is as indispensable to a magazine as it is to sane living."

In this, editor Cousins conforms to a long tradition of media spoofing.

One of the best-known media in-games has been played for decades by Al Hirschfeld, the well-known theatrical cartoonist, and readers of the *New York Times*'s Sunday drama section. Hidden within those clever cartoons is the name of Mr. Hirschfeld's daughter Nina. The name masquerades as folds of cloth, facial wrinkles, or strands of hair.

"Finding the Nina's" is one of the great joys of Hirschfeld buffs. "Look for the crossbar in the *A*," is their hint to novices. Beside his signature the cartoonist obligingly notes the number of "Nina's" in each illustration, an indication of this in-game's popularity.

Cartoonists are among the most mischievous in-joke players, the lightheartedness of their output giving them fairly free rein.

Through the years the home swamp of Pogo, that little possum, has received a parade of prominent visitors. They have included a sinister-looking bobcat called Simple J. Malarkey (strong resemblances to Senator Joseph R. McCarthy), a pig-and-parrot pair not unlike Khrushchev and Bulganin, and a Lyndon Johnson–like Texas longhorn steer. The late Walt Kelly, who created the strip, is said to have complained privately that readers too often failed to get these political in-jokes.

While thousands of people participate in some media

in-games, others are subtle and exclusive. The players may be only a small group of people.

ESCAPE? FEW DO

The byline "Harrison Albany," for example, used to raise smiles among staffers of Boston's *Herald-American*. The paper's editorial offices happen to be at Harrison and Albany streets.

Hardly a publication anywhere has escaped being used for this kind of in-game. But such games sometimes go awry, especially when they are played on inappropriate terrain. The news columns of the *New York Times*, which considers itself a newspaper of record, is inappropriate terrain.

In June 1966, a young *Times* man submitted a story covering a college commencement. Among the long list of distinctions was one titled the "Brett Award." According to the writer's copy it had been won by "Jake Barnes." The inclusion of this fictitious award and its winner, alluding to characters in Ernest Hemingway's novel *The Sun Also Rises*, did not amuse the paper's editors. The reporter lost his job.

Media spoofs give editors and readers a chance to laugh at themselves and the preconceptions they share. The appearances of Dr. Grant Swinger, director of the Center for the Absorption of Federal Funds, is always an event for readers of *Science and Government Report*, a Washington-based newsletter on science policy. In a recent interview Dr. Swinger explained the work of his center. It aimed to support public understanding of science, he stated, so that "the man on the street won't mistake stannous fluoride for a Russian novelist."

Justifying Dr. Swinger's appearances, Daniel Greenberg, the report's editor, comments: "Some of this field [science and public policy] is so absurd that if you handle it in regular ways you're not performing a service for your readers. Swinger's known throughout the scientific world," he adds. "Whenever we publish a piece about him, we get requests for it from all over the world."

Herewith some "Personals" items from the pages of the *Saturday Review.* K. Jason Sitewell was the author of many of them.

WOULD ANY sporting goods manufacturer be interested in helping me patent a golf ball which, upon being hit, emits a low moan fully expressive of the suffering of the average golfer upon completing his swing? The sound of anguish is fully audible up to 175 yards from the tee. Box S176.

THROUGH AN UNTOWARD HAPPENSTANCE I am unable to understand, a packet of 17 torrid love letters was placed in my overcoat pocket while it hung in the clothes rack on American Airlines flight 489 from Dallas to Columbus, Ohio, on March 21. My home situation would be greatly improved if the person who mistakenly deposited this packet would step forward and claim same. By an abominable coincidence my name is also Irving. SR Box IA.

IRVING. Please forgive me for having stashed the love letters in your overcoat pocket on flight 489 from Dallas to Columbus. I had to get rid of them very quickly but never would have done it to you if I had known your name was also Irving. Honest. Hope this squares things at home. Contritely. Irving B.

EARNEST YOUNG MAN with deep interest in the Polish marshes and a yen for veal scallopini would like to hear from compatible parties. SR Box SV.

GERALDINE: Valentine's Day is our day, despite all the busybodies. I'll be outside the wig shop at noon. You'll be able to identify me by the heart on my sleeve. Seymour.

I HAVE COME INTO POSSESSION of toupee believed to have been worn and lost by William Howard Taft for three-week period during Presidential campaign of 1908. What am I offered? SR Box TW.

GERALDINE: The reason why I wasn't in front of the wig shop on Valentine's Day was that I turned my ankle on those damned hilly Seattle streets and had to have it bandaged. By the time I got there you were gone. Anyway, I love you and need you and just pray that your husband understands. Seymour.

SEYMOUR: I tried it out on my husband. No soap. What do we do now? Geraldine.

GERALDINE: I have just discovered that your husband is really my half-brother Morty who disappeared eight years ago. You can tell by the large mole on his left shoulder. This complicates matters; we had better call it off. Seymour.

SEYMOUR: I'm not going to let Morty's mole get in the way of our beautiful relationship. Where are you? Geraldine.

GERALDINE: I still love you but you've got to decide between Morty and his mole and me. Seymour.

EAGER TO FIND a publisher for my manuscript "I Was the Mother of Adolf Hitler's Secret Child Bride." SR Box IA.

WILL THE YOUNG LADY who dismounted from the bus at Peoria, failing to return but leaving me to guard her pregnant dachshund, please communicate with me soonest. What do I do with the pups? SR Box DD.

TO MY THREE SONS AND TWO DAUGHTERS: Eighteen years of unexplained absence is a long time, but I am now back and eager to tell you what happened. Please let me know where you are. Your loving father, R.E.T., Jr. SR Box TE.

WILL THE LADY who asked me to mind her parrot and ironing board at the O'Hare Airport in Chicago and then forgot to come back, please claim same. The parrot squawks constantly and my wife is on my neck. SR Box WD.

WHAT AM I OFFERED for parrot that imitates George Burns but speaks only between 3 and 5 A.M.? SR Box BG.

COMPUTER ERROR HAS CAUSED us to manufacture 320 marine compasses, needles pointing West only. Strictly for the weekend mariner who knows his way about. Westroads Marine Compass Co. SR Box BB.

BAR STOOL from which President James K. Polk was believed to have fallen while visiting Marine Tavern in 1846. Bids accepted. SR Box CY.

MADELEINE, the crate of live lobsters has been returned with an "address unknown" sticker. Where are you? Casper.

32

TO THE 130 students and travelers who were stranded in New Zealand in September 1966 when our steamship ran aground and who have not yet returned to the U.S. We are informed by our legal counsel that our liability is limited to cost of a one-way fare and does not apply to living expenses incurred during the period of residence in New Zealand. Worldover Travel. SR Box QV.

WE REGRET MISLABELING ERROR that has resulted in our laundry soap flakes being packaged in boxes carrying shredded wheat labels. This warning does not apply to North Dakota and Montana where old supply is still adequate. Refunds cheerfully made. Everight Soap Company. SR Box SE.

ENHANCE YOUR WATER BED with our fountain attachment that will produce five-foot multicolored spouts. Comes with decorative basin with recirculating feature. SR Box WB.

I AM CAPABLE OF ELEGANT and soaring thoughts under the gentle stimulus of a South Pacific island sun. Is any book publisher curious about my unborn masterpiece? SR Box SP.

NOTICE TO ALL BUYERS OF OUR MANUAL, *Guide to Levitation.* We sincerely apologize for the incorrect use of the word "levitation" in our title instead of the correct word, "levity"—a mistake readily apparent to any reader of the table of contents. Requests for refunds will be promptly honored. SR Box LG.

JUST RECEIVED FRESH SHIPMENT of mitigated gall from peachable pastries. First come, first served. SR Box MG.

ARE YOU LOSING OUT because you are making yourself too clear? We can help give you an impressive ambiguity that can command the respectful attention and admiration of your colleagues, customers, and business associates. SR Box LO.

ALIBIS FOR EVERY OCCASION: Full range of original excuses, all the way from what to say to your boss if he finds your unflattering caricatures of him on your doodle pad, to a surefire explanation for your wife if she finds panty hose other than her own in the glove compartment of your car. Survival Through Mendacity, Inc. SR Box AF.

OUR APOLOGIES TO ALL THOSE who ordered *Origins of the Italian Renaissance,* and who received our 12-volume set instead on the *Mating Habits of Afghanistan Tribes.* Full refunds cheer-

fully provided. 21st Century Books. SR Box 1R.

I WOULD LIKE to go around the world and promise to write fascinating and luminous letters about it in exchange for tickets and other expenses. SR Box KJS.

WE WISH TO APOLOGIZE publicly to the 796 members of the World Stamp Collector's Society who went to Norwalk, Connecticut, instead of Norwalk, California, for our annual convention because of printer's error on invitation. M. G. Stuckey, President WSCS. SR Box AC.

SHALL I BRING my catamite to the party? This and other questions are answered in our new *Guide to Social Etiquette.* SR Box CO.

UNFORTUNATE COMPUTER ERROR has resulted in

large quantities of egg benders with reverse effect; i.e., they liquefy rather than increase density of foods. Bids sought. SR Box EB.

SPONTANEOUS QUIPS FURNISHED to political candidates. Can be droll or abusive to suit unlimited temperaments. Coaching obtainable if required. SR Box PC.

WE APOLOGIZE TO ALL OUR MEMBERS who went to Moscow, U.S.S.R. instead of Moscow, Idaho, for our annual convention because of unfortunate typographical error in our April 1978 *Bulletin.* International Trampoline Association. SR Box AC.

EAGER TO DISPOSE OF 8,000 color-decorated paper towels that, due to unfortunate computer error, have slightly sandpapered surface. Bids accepted. SR Box PT.

COMPUTER ERROR responsible for 700 dozen undersized egg cups— excellent buy for pigeon-egg fanciers. Inquire SR Box PE.

IRENE: Please listen to me: I didn't do it; my dachshund did. Tell me where you are. SR Box IL.

NOTICE: Our traveling medical clinic is now starting on its national tour and will be available to treat your golf-related illnesses and psychiatric problems caused by golf. Write for itinerary. K. Jason Sitewell, Inc. SR Box GI.

COMPUTER ERROR has resulted in large supply of electric-powered swivel chairs that make approximately 150 high-speed revolutions per minute automatically as soon as body weight hits the seat. Excellent bargain for people who are nausea-resistant. SR Box SC.

WONDERING WHAT TO DO if your water bed freezes this winter? Our trained hamsters (sold in pairs only) skate for hours to the tune of the beautiful "Blue Danube" waltz. Pair sold complete with 33 LP record and 8 extra miniature skates. WM Box D.

NOW SPACE AGE technology makes it possible for you to avoid those frenetic runs to the kitchen during the TV commercials. Our combination TV- refrigerator keeps you where the action is. Single unit in gleaming white adds to decor of any living room. WM Box ML.

ORPHANS, VISITING out-of-towners, don't miss the fun. Our service supplies a parent on an hourly basis so that you can get to see *those* movies. WM Box SC.

FILM BUFFS: Stills wanted. Will trade set from *White Queen of the Bantus* (di-

rected, 1931, by Mansfield McGraw) for any from three films directed by Rodney Pomerantz— 1930–32, RKO. Preferred: *Rendezvous in Pittsburgh.* WM Box RC1.

NOTICE: Due to circumstances beyond our control, the forty-second annual reunion of the Vestal Virgins of America Society will not be held this year. Cynthia P. Cartwright, President.

BUSINESSMEN: ARE YOUR OFFICE visitors slow in leaving after they've completed their business? Our manual provides your secretary with 24 surefire urgent messages—useful for terminating virtually any unduly prolonged conversations. WM Box NF.

YOUNG, EXTRAORDINARILY INTELLIGENT, handsome, wealthy young man seeks correspondence with young girl not obsessed by women's lib and who doesn't resent her mother for adoring and taking good care of her father. WM Box OE.

IMPORTANT NOTICE: If you are one of the hundreds of parachuting enthusiasts who bought our course entitled "Easy Sky Diving in One Fell Swoop," please make the following correction: On page 8, line 7, change "state zip code" to "pull rip cord."

3

Congressman
A. F. Day
and H.R. 6142

The letters' page of *SR* was more than a repository for comments on material appearing in the magazine. It provided a catharsis for our readers on all sorts of deep concerns. Thus it was that we published a communication from Mr. Sitewell, the urgent tone of which seemed to the editors to warrant substantial space. In the weeks following publication of this letter, the tally of mail to Congress showed that the bill introduced by Congressman A. F. Day was not going by unnoticed, as had been feared by K.

Jason Sitewell. It was perhaps only coincidental that K.J.S.'s letter appeared, as did so many other communications from him, in the first issue in April.

Letters to the Editor

A CALL TO DEFEAT H.R. 6142

Sir:

Over the years, the editors of *SR* have championed the most significant causes of our time.

I now come before you with another cause that I trust you will not regard as too inconsequential to warrant the kind of personal eloquence that has been so characteristic of your editorial page. I refer to the need to defeat House Resolution 6142, introduced by Representative A. F. Day and cosponsored by some forty members of the House. This bill, which for some inexplicable reason has received virtually no attention, would abolish all privately owned parks of more than 50 acres and all public recreational areas or grounds of more than 150 acres that are used by fewer than 150 persons per day, averaged over a week.

The bill sounds democratic enough until one recognizes that its principal effect would be to eliminate the nation's golf courses. This is not the stated purpose, of course, but it would certainly be the principal effect.

The minimal amount of land required even for a private 9-hole course is 75 acres. Most country clubs, with their 18-hole courses, occupy more than 200 acres. By definition, therefore, all private golf facilities would be closed.

What about public golf courses? The average public

golf course, running between 175 and 250 acres, is played on by fewer than 150 persons a day, averaged over the week. This average is made up of about 400 playing on Saturdays and Sundays and 60 playing on weekdays. Congressman Day very cleverly specified "fewer than 150 persons per day, averaged out over a week." There is not a public golf course in the country that would not be shut down under this definition.

I believe I can prove that Congressman Day is deliberately seeking to destroy golf. Permit me to speak personally, I have known A. F. Day since childhood. We grew up in Los Angeles together. We went to the same public elementary school in Brentwood. In our eighth-grade English class, we had to write a five-hundred-word essay on the subject: "What is the first thing you would do if you were president?" Day's little composition, which was not a joke, said the first thing he would do as president would be to abolish golf. He wrote that it was worse than alcohol as a disruptive influence within the family.

What Day's classmates didn't realize at the time was that he was writing out of his own tragic family experience. His grandfather perished in a sand trap on the 5th hole of the public course at Hillsborough, California, the victim of a heart attack caused by massive exasperation and exhaustion. Day's father was fired from at least three jobs because he persisted in goofing off for golf. The family never saw Mr. Day on weekends. He would leave the house before 4 A.M. in order to wait on line for a starting time. After each game, he would go to the clubhouse bar and recapitulate the entire game, stroke by stroke, with his cronies. He played miserably. It was not at all unusual for him to have several 5-putt greens per game. He anguished over every slice and hook. All this added up to a great deal of anguish. His blood pressure was almost as high as his score. He would have golf nightmares in which he would have 6-putt greens. He would take grocery money away from the family to buy expensive golf equipment.

Inevitably, Day became unemployable. Just as inevitably, he developed a serious case of hypertension and ulcers. One day, playing at San Jose, not far from the site of the grandfather's tragedy, Day expired from a coronary undoubtedly caused by his uncontrollable frenzy after hitting nineteen successive balls into the pond in front of a par-3 green. Little wonder that the son should have developed such a fierce antipathy to the game.

We went to UCLA together. In our senior year, A. F. Day wrote a term paper for our economics course that clearly reflected his embittered feelings about the sport. His paper differed from the one he wrote in the eighth grade only in its additional sophistication. He used ostensibly detailed research to disguise his psychotic hostility. His paper revealed that in just one year 18,000 men died on golf courses from heart attacks; 72,000 men developed ulcers or gastritis from acute anguish over their inability to hit the ball properly; 930 men were killed and 8,600 were injured in overturned golf carts. His paper further disclosed that golf was the principal cause each year of more than 60,000 broken homes; that it was by far the greatest single cause of alcoholism and acute melancholy in the United States; that it kept 3,642,000 acres— twice as much acreage as that devoted to the national forests—out of productive cultivation or from other important social duties, of which low-cost housing was the most conspicuous.

Our economics professor at UCLA was not impressed by Day's paper. He thought it capricious and unworthy, and said so. Day never forgave him and gloated when the professor broke his collarbone in a golf-cart accident only three days after giving Day a failing grade. When Day was elected to Congress three years ago, I naturally wondered how his malicious obsession would manifest itself. Now I know. But what about the forty-three congressmen who have announced their support for Day's bill? Do they know? Day's bill is all dressed up in the ecological and conservationist fashion of the day. It is made to appear that the bill will protect what are cleverly described as private parks, ensuring their use for the public good. For those congressmen whose constituencies consist largely of the poorly housed or impoverished, the bill holds out the prospect of low-cost housing in verdant settings.

A. F. Day is not the first man elected to public office in our history who has been motivated and energized by a secret or absurd purpose. It is a terrible error to underestimate him. I regret deeply having to make all this known, but history has often been twisted all out of shape because not enough people took seriously a few men who acted out of their obsessions or deep-seated aversions.

I urge *SR*'s editors to oppose H.R. 6142; I urge all your readers, especially those who regard golf not as a vicious and extravagant diversion but as a prime manifestation of the American way of life, to write to their congressman making known the real facts about Congressman Day's bill. Everyone who knows what weekends are for has the obligation now to act.

K. Jason Sitewell
Burlingame, Calif.

EDITOR'S NOTE: A copy of this letter has been sent to Congressman Day, who has requested space for a reply. His letter will appear next week.

CONGRESSMAN DAY DEFENDS HIMSELF

Sir:

K. Jason Sitewell, in "A Call to Defeat H.R. 6142" [*SR*, April 3], makes it appear that the bill I introduced in the House of Representatives has a secret and pernicious purpose. He says I am dominated by a "malicious obsession" to destroy golf.

The forty-three members of the House who are co-sponsoring my bill will bear witness to the fact that I have never made any secret of my opposition to privileged use of parks, public or private. I believe it is undemocratic and indeed arrogant for large tracts of land to be pre-empted by small numbers of people for any purpose, be it golf or any other so-called sport. I have no objection to public golf courses so long as they are used by enough people to justify the public taxes that support them. Admittedly, it is difficult to define "reasonable use" in terms of numbers of people involved. Arbitrarily, perhaps, I have hit on an average of 150 persons per day as a reasonable number. Any public golf course that is used by more than this number of people has nothing to fear from my bill. Private courses, of course, will not be exempt.

I trust this sets the record straight so far as my purposes and objectives are concerned. Now let me raise some questions about K. Jason Sitewell and the *Saturday Review*.

Mr. Sitewell says he has known me since early childhood. That is correct. Obviously, therefore, my own knowledge of him is of equal duration. Would it surprise the readers of *SR* to learn that Mr. Sitewell is one of the largest investors in sporting-goods equipment in the country?

Now for *SR:* I am sure the magazine's readers must find it strange that Mr. Sitewell's letter appeared in *SR.* The letters page is usually reserved for comment on material that has previously appeared in the magazine. The Sitewell letter was totally unrelated to any earlier article in *SR.* Yet the editor gave it a full page. Why? I point a finger at the editor himself.

The public image of N.C. is of a man dedicated to literature, philosophy, and important public causes. He has been known as a confidant of such men as Schweitzer, Nehru, President John F. Kennedy, and Pope John XXIII. This is not the real N.C. The real N.C. became revealed to me the other night when I listened to Arnold Palmer on the "Tonight" show. Palmer spoke of playing golf with his "good friend Norman Cousins" and of dedicating his latest golf book to him. The next day I obtained a copy of the book. There it was, the reference to the editor of *SR* as a golf-playing buddy. Good Lord! The next thing we know, Spiro Agnew will be writing editorials for *The Saturday Review! Sic transit gloria mundi.*

A. F. Day
House Office Building
Washington, D.C.

Nothing happened, at least not right away, after the publication of K.J.S.'s poignant plea to defeat Congressman Day's nefarious bill. But his letter served as the basis for animated comment by a number of newspaper sportswriters. One of the nation's leading golf magazines reprinted K.J.S.'s letter under a double-spread headline: "A FRIGHT-

ENING BILL." The result of these alarming stories and editorials was that the governing committees of country clubs across the country sprang to action. The editor of the *Saturday Review* was obsessed by the conceit that he could shoot in the low eighties, a wish devoutly to be consummated. The manager of the golf course in Connecticut that suffered N.C.'s misguided efforts informed him of a special meeting of the board of governors, called for the purpose of mapping the club's strategy to defeat H.R. 6142. Even after N.C. stripped away K.J.S.'s disguise and laid bare the nature of the plot, the club manager set his jaw and said he would go through with the meeting anyway—just to be sure. With or without respect to the Connecticut sector, the protest over A. F. Day's bill rose day by day, as the following pages reveal.

Sir:

As a member of the House Republican leadership I would like to express my unequivocal opposition to H.R. 6142 as introduced by Congressman A. F. Day (D-Calif.), along with forty-three House cosponsors. And I want to make it perfectly clear from the outset that I do not play golf, nor do I have any vested interest in private golf clubs.

The ostensible purpose of H.R. 6142 is to eliminate those open spaces which are either being used as privileged recreation sanctuaries by the affluent or are being underused as recreation areas by the general public, thus freeing these areas for other purposes and wider public usage. While the Day bill, on its face, would seem to have the greatest good for the greatest number in mind, I would submit that a closer view will reveal that there is nothing great or good about this legislation, and that future generations will suffer if it is passed. It is obvious that if this legislation is enacted, these open spaces will be immediately converted into housing developments and shopping centers, and their verdant value and beauty will be lost forever.

This legislation runs completely contrary to the president's "Legacy of Parks" program as outlined in his environment message of February 15, 1971. The "Legacy of Parks" program is aimed at both preserving and expanding urban open space, recreation, wilderness, and other natural areas. As the president pointed out in his message, the demand for such areas continues to accelerate. With growing population and leisure time, Congressman Day's bill would take us in the opposite direction by diminishing rather than increasing such areas. In the president's words: "Only if we set aside and develop such recreation areas now can we ensure that they will be available for future generations."

With best wishes I am,

Very truly yours,
John B. Anderson
Member of Congress
Washington, D.C.

[N.B. This is the same John B. Anderson who campaigned for the presidency in 1980.]

ॐ

Dear Mr. Cousins:

Imagine my embarrassment when members kept calling me at home or stopping me in the Club rooms to ask, "What is your relationship to A. F. Day?"

Exhaustedly yours,

R. D. Day, Jr., President
Richmond Times-Dispatch

When the controversy over A. F. Day and his bill to abolish golf approached its crescendo, *SR*'s editor received a call from the *Wall Street Journal.* Who was K. Jason Sitewell? Where did he get his facts? And where could he be reached? It was clear by now that the entire matter had gotten out of hand. We decided to play it straight. The *Wall Street Journal* exposed the spoof.

The first part of the story was matter-of-fact. It merely quoted from K.J.S.'s letter as it appeared in *SR.* Any hint of a spoof was deferred to the continuation of the story on the back pages. As is well known, the human race is divided into two groups: those who jump to the back of the newspaper to read continuations, and those who don't. In the case of *WSJ,* those who didn't jumped into the fight, which started up the mail to the Congress all over again. But among those who did jump to the back of the paper was the editor of the golf magazine that reprinted Mr. Sitewell's original letter. Understandably, he was livid. He felt that no punishment, however severe, would be adequate, and he proposed that *SR*'s editor be barred for life from the nation's golf courses. I was deeply moved by his outrage and replied that I was properly contrite, recognizing that punishment was in order; but I didn't feel that the proposed measure would have the desired effect, for if they really knew how much I suffered playing golf, they not only would permit me to play but insist that I be allowed to play through.

A FRIGHTENING BILL

In a long letter to the editor in the April 3 issue of *Saturday Review*, K. Jason Sitewell bitterly attacked a bill proposed by Congressman A. F. Day that would have the effect of outlawing all golf courses, public and private.

What the bill (House Resolution 6142) would do, Sitewell explained, would be to abolish all privately owned parks of more than 50 acres and all public recreation areas of more than 150 acres that are used by fewer than 150 persons a day.

Sitewell declared that Congressman Day had long held the view that golf is an economic waste and a cause of broken homes, premature deaths, disabling injuries, and a land shortage.

The reason for Day's hatred of golf was explained by the fact that his grandfather "perished in a sand trap on the 5th hole of the public course at Hillsborough, California, the victim of a heart attack caused by massive exasperation and exhaustion." A few years later, Day's father "expired from a coronary undoubtedly caused by his uncontrollable frenzy after hitting nineteen successive balls into the pond in front of a par-3 green."

In the *Saturday Review* the following week, Representative Day answered Sitewell, citing the latter as being "one of the largest investors in sporting-goods equipment in the country."

As a result of the publicity given to Day's bill—which had not received any prior public notice—some golf clubs made plans to fight the measure, outraged golfers wrote to members of Congress, a sports columnist for a Chicago paper denounced Day's "obfuscatory thinking that confuses commonweal with eradication of private enterprise and ownership," and a national golf weekly denounced Day in an editorial headed "A Frightening Bill."

Well, it turned out—as the *Wall Street Journal* explains in a delightful story on the subject—that A. F. Day meant April Fool's Day, and that the Sitewell letter and the Day follow-up were creatures of the imagination of *Saturday Review* editor Norman Cousins.

We sympathize with those who were "taken in" by the spoof, and are happy we weren't among them. But such April Fool's fantasias are a tradition at *Saturday Review,* and they are to be lauded, as long as nobody really gets hurt. For, as editor Cousins says, "We like to laugh and share our laughter with others, especially in times when there's not much to laugh about."

And April 1971 does seem to be one of those times.

Article by Jim Bergman of *The Saturday Evening Post*

GOLF'S FINEST HOUR

This story is dedicated to the many thousands of American golfers who in 1971 mounted one of the largest protest campaigns in the history of the United States. It matters little that the proposed antigolf legislation that they were protesting was a hoax, or that each and every one was acting out the part of an April fool. What really matters is that our country's duffers proved their ability to mobilize and act effectively on a national scale when the future of their sport was so obviously threatened.

K. Jason Sitewell was beside himself with worry. The

bill recently introduced by Congressman A. F. Day and cosponsored by forty-three other representatives had received virtually no attention from the media. Unless the public was alerted, and alerted right away, House Resolution 6142 would become the law of the land and the nation's golf courses would be converted into either verdant settings for low-cost housing or pleasure parks for family picnickers.

So Sitewell sat down in the living room of his modest bungalow in Burlingame, California, and pondered what action he should take. A few minutes later the light bulb inside his mind exploded. Why not write a letter about Representative Day and his nefarious bill to *Saturday Review,* the highbrow weekly magazine based in New York City? After all, the main reason he had subscribed to the magazine since 1942, the year Norman Cousins became its editor, was his admiration of *Saturday Review*'s unflinching editorial courage in tackling the most complex and important issues of our time—nuclear disarmament, effective world government, air pollution, and the dispensing of unsafe drugs, to name just a few. And while Sitewell did not always agree with the magazine's stand on each and every issue, he felt assured that it would welcome the opportunity to add this spurious attempt to destroy one of the country's most wholesome avocations to its long list of worthy campaigns.

Sitewell composed the letter with great deliberation, double-checking all facts and carefully avoiding any exaggeration or inflammatory language so that Day's supporters could not later accuse him of unfair bias. . . . It had taken Sitewell three painstaking hours to write the letter, but the effort paid off handsomely when the *Saturday Review* of April 3, 1971, published it in full. The letter, which ran to well over one thousand words, took up an entire page of the magazine's "Letters to the Editor" section. Sitewell sat back and waited confidently for public indignation to snowball into a national protest campaign. A week passed, and absolutely nothing happened. "Has the world gone mad?" he asked himself.

Then, in the April 10 issue of *Saturday Review,* a reply from Rep. A. F. Day appeared. To no one's surprise, the congressman denied that he was driven by a "malicious obsession" to destroy golf. In fact, the charge was so preposterous that Representative Day did not even bother to mention the golf-related family tragedies which Sitewell had disclosed in his letter. . . .

Golfdom's hierarchy swiftly teed up for action. Boards of governors and executive committees of golf clubs from coast to coast called emergency meetings to plot strategy against H.R. 6142. Members with friends and acquaintances in government were delegated to solicit their support. There was even talk of raising money for the ensuing battle and of staging media-catching demonstrations.

Nor were the rank and file of America's duffers idle. Many actually gave up Sunday playing time to stay at home with their families and write letters of protest to newspapers, magazines, and their congressmen. Within two weeks of the publication of an editorial on the subject in *Golf World,* an estimated 19,000 letters of protest had poured into congressional offices, thereby catapulting the Day bill into the list of top ten domestic issues. House Minority Leader Gerald Ford received a letter from a constituent who conceded that "anyone would sympathize with Representative Day's family tragedy," but nonetheless urged the congressman to vote against H.R. 6142.

51

Confusion and ugly recriminations reigned in the nation's capital. Congressmen beseeched by angry voters stalled for time while their staffs made the necessary inquiries. An aide to Senator Harry F. Byrd of Virginia, replying to a letter from a constituent, wrote that while it was "somewhat premature for the senator to take a stand," the bill would seem to have only a "slim chance" of passing. An ugly rumor that Vice-President Spiro T. Agnew's recent antics on various golf courses had reactivated Representative Day's traumatic childhood memories swept rapidly through the city. And many Washingtonians had visions of irate golfers streaming into the capital by the thousands and golf-carting down Pennsylvania Avenue in protest against the Day Bill.

Fortunately, it never came to that. On April 12, the *Wall Street Journal* carried a front-page article by W. Steward Pinkerton, Jr., which revealed that H.R. 6142 was in reality a bill dealing with the liability of national banks for certain taxes, and that Representative A. F. Day (full name: April Fool's Day) and K. Jason Sitewell (an imperfect anagram for "Well, it's a joke, son") were pen names adopted by the editor of *Saturday Review*. Norman Cousins had perpetrated a gigantic spoof which probably frightened more people than Orson Welles's radio play, *The War of the Worlds*. . . .

To those who condemn the hoax as a "cruel, distorted idea of a joke," Norman Cousins points to the fundamental difference between a spoof and a practical joke. "A spoof has some underlying significance and is actually nourishing to all concerned," he argues. "A practical joke, on the other hand, is mean, easy to do, and hurtful." . . .

For many April fools, however, the line between a

spoof and a practical joke is either invisible or downright irrelevant. But many who disliked the hoax also found merit in the reaction it fostered. *Golf World* magazine, for instance, chose to bask in the one ray of sunshine generated by the spoof. "If for some pseudoecological reason golf courses become threatened," wrote Richard Taylor, "it appears that the world of golf is ready for action."

That, as we now know, is an understatement of colossal dimensions.

Personals

PUBLIC NOTICE: We are withdrawing from circulation the manual *Moth-Training Made Easy.* Reports from readers indicate 15 to 20 percent of trained moths attack their masters. No need for alarm; moth bites may be painful but are not poisonous. As soon as our moth experts find out what has gone wrong, we will return your book with further instructions. Moth Specialties Co., New York, N.Y.

IT'S SANDAL TIME AGAIN. Are your feet pretty enough to let you face this season without embarrassment? If not, we have the perfect answer. Our vinyl pullovers give you beautiful bare feet that can't be detected from the real thing. And best of all, they come with or without arch supports. Please specify size, color of skin, and gender desired. Ten-Toes, Inc. WM Box TZ.

INSOMNIA A PROBLEM? Fall asleep instantly by listening to our LP recordings of congressional roll-call votes. Write: Surplus

Sound Co., c/o SR/W Box WG.

DO YOU HAVE TROUBLE getting service in restaurants? Do you sit for hours while waitresses ignore you? Our flashing, portable, self-powered 18″ Beacon Light can be set up instantly. SR/W Box BB.

4

More Things You Never Knew about Golf

AND WOULD JUST AS SOON FORGET

Golf Digest magazine, mindful of K. Jason Sitewell's interest in golf, invited K.J.S. to contribute an annual article celebrating the sport in its April issues. K.J.S. accepted the invitation and kept the series going for several years.

THE GREATEST FEAT
IN THE HISTORY OF GOLF

The beginning of April marks the seventy-fifth anniversary of what is probably the most spectacular feat in the history of golf. The records are uncertain whether it was

March 31, 1900, or the next day (the only living witness of the event claims it was the latter).

It happened at the Imperial Golf Club in Melbourne, Australia. The principal characters were A. F. Daye, the leading British professional of his time, and Langley Corrigan, the local golf champion and winner of the Australian Open in 1899.

Both men were touring Australia in a head-to-head series. The match at Melbourne brought out a record crowd. Three matches had been played prior to Melbourne, Corrigan winning two of them. The people of the area were ablaze with excitement over the prospect that the local favorite would triumph over the vaunted Britisher.

The Melbourne course was a good test. Par, 73. Length, 7,900 yards. The toughest hole was the par-3 number 17, reminiscent of the famous over-the-water 16th at Cypress Point in California, where many pros accept bogeys with equanimity if not a spirit of thanksgiving. When players approach the 17th at Melbourne, they are close to a precipice; the drop to the floor of the canyon is about 1,200 feet. The green is 215 yards away. Usually, a strong wind whips in from the sea. Some of the longest hitters in golf have challenged the hole with a driver and fallen far short.

On this particular day, Al Daye was 1-up coming to the 17th. Corrigan was the first to hit (in those days, the player who was behind in the match always hit first). Playing it safe, Corrigan hit a 3-iron into the wind to the dogleg fairway on the short side of the gap about 170 yards away. He seemed certain to get no better than a bogey.

Daye saw a chance to wrap up the match right then.

He was a long-ball hitter, outdriving Corrigan by 20 yards or more on most of the tee shots. He took out his 3-wood and challenged the canyon. The ball started out like a cannon shot; it appeared certain it would carry the green. When the ball reached its peak about 170 yards out, however, it hit galelike reverse winds and fell about 10 yards short, plopping down to the canyon floor. Knowing he had lost the hole anyway, and being stubborn, Daye took out his driver and belted a prodigious second shot that on an ordinary day would have carried at least 280 yards. The winds were now full force in the faces of the players and the ball fell short again—this time by only 6 or 7 feet. Daye decided on a third try—teed up, fired, and missed.

Now the gale hit in full fury. Daye's caddie, an Australian aborigine of sixty-one years who couldn't have weighed more than 105 pounds, did something most unusual. He asked for permission to hit a ball over the ravine. Daye promptly put down a ball and offered his number-1 wood, which the caddie spurned. All this time he had been carrying what appeared to be a walking stick. He turned it around and took a swipe at the ball which he had teed up very low. The swing was entirely original. The aborigine stood about 10 feet to the rear of the ball and then appeared to run at it, lashing at it with terrific velocity. It was a low wind-cheating shot and easily made the green despite the long yardage.

Everyone was thunderstruck. When Daye recovered, he teed up a ball and invited the old man to hit again. Once again, the caddie ran at the ball like a javelin thrower, flinging himself at it, then springing into the air, at the second of impact. This time, the ball was lost in the deepening fog and rain. No one knew whether it made the green.

The entire party started out for the other side, walking around the semi-horseshoe of the landscape to the green. When they got to the green, no ball was to be seen. The area around the green was flat and open; no ball there either.

Then, suddenly, Corrigan began shouting incoherently. He was holding the pin and jumping up and down. Daye rushed up to Corrigan and demanded to know what the shouting was about. Still yelling, Corrigan jabbed at the hole with the pin. Daye looked down. Two balls were in the cup. Daye bent down to the balls, then looked up and smiled to the crowd. These were the two balls he had given the old man. Two successive holes-in-one by the same player on the same hole! Nothing like it had ever happened before (or has happened since). What made it all the more incredible was that it was done with a stick hardly the size of a walking cane. It later developed that the aborigine, whose name was Vrootengrud, had never played with regular clubs. He had used his cane for everything except putting.

As the result of Vrootengrud's double hole-in-one, hundreds of golfers would pilgrimage early in April each year to the site of the 17th tee. They would congregate close to the precipice, and hold a sort of Quaker meeting, one of their number painstakingly recounting the episode. Inevitably, over the years, the story was embellished.

One version described Vrootengrud as being ten or fifteen years older than listed. In another version, his son was the caddie and the old man was trailing along with the crowd, hobbling along on a cane, then stepping forward after Daye gave up, turning his cane around and bashing two balls across the long ravine into the teeth of the gale. According to this version, Vrootengrud announced his feat in advance, much in the manner of Babe Ruth pointing to the bleachers just before swatting a home run against Chicago in 1932.

But these versions are plainly apocryphal. The true story is good enough just as it is and requires no embroidery.

The annual pilgrimages ceased with World War I in 1914. By that time the memory of the Vrootengrud feat had begun to recede. But a marble stone was erected at the site of the 17th tee memorializing the event. And the *Australian Sportsman,* which comes out the first of each month, publishes a short annual reminder of the event in its April issue. Last year, for example, the magazine ran a box in its editorial page, which I reproduce herewith:

VROOTENGRUD RECALLED

Seventy-four years ago on this date, the most spectacular feat in the history of golf, two successive holes-in-one, was performed by a caddie, Vrootengrud, believed to be 61 years old at the time. We honor his memory for the glory he has eternally brought to Melbourne.

The Vrootengrud legend is only slightly tarnished by something that came to light in 1905. Everyone had assumed at first that Vrootengrud had performed his feat with an ordinary walking cane, hitting the ball with the handle. Actually, he had used an authentic golf club of the variety in use during the early years of golf in Scotland; that is, a straight branch with a crooked neck. Vrootengrud had fashioned the club when he began to caddie as a youth of thirteen and played with it regularly. After he turned fifty he became slightly arthritic and used the club as a cane.

It is not precisely accurate, therefore, to say that he hit his successive holes-in-one with a walking stick. Just the same, the truth detracts very little from the achievement. Even if he had made his successive holes-in-one with a modern graphite club, it still would have to be regarded as probably the most amazing achievement in the history of any sport.

About Vrootengrud himself: his glory, in a sense, turned out to be his undoing. Many players wanted to be able to boast they had been caddied by an old man who had performed a golfing miracle. Despite his worsening arthritis, Vrootengrud tried to accommodate everyone who asked for him—not charging anything extra even though he could easily have cashed in on his fame. His infirmity increased with the years, but he persisted nevertheless.

As might be expected, every time the players for whom he was caddying came to the 17th hole, Vrootengrud was asked to reproduce his feat. The old man was smart enough to beg off. He kept at his job until four days before his death at the age of seventy-seven. The obituary in the *A.S.* gave the date of death as August 9, 1916.

To the end, Vrootengrud's only goal in life was to be a good caddie. That he achieved his purpose there can be no doubt.

THE ASTOUNDING STORY
OF THE GOLFING GORILLAS

I have a Danish friend who is the director of the Royal Copenhagen Zoo—one of the world's best. About ten years ago my friend came to the United States on a tour of American zoos. He was especially impressed with the show the gorillas and chimpanzees put on at the St. Louis Zoo—riding motorcycles and doing circus acts. My friend hired the young assistant trainer at the St. Louis Zoo and brought him to Copenhagen for the purpose of developing a chimpanzee-and-gorilla act that would be a prime tourist attraction.

My friend succeeded. Within three years the primates at the Royal Copenhagen Zoo could put on a performance that was unsurpassed anywhere in the world. Not even the St. Louis Zoo could match it. Chimpanzees did high-wire acts, typed words called out by people in the audience, and played the guitar. One gorilla executed a perfect reverse two-and-a-half from the high diving board.

Three years ago, I visited my zoo-keeping Danish friend. The next day we played golf at the Royal Deer Park Golf Course just outside Copenhagen. He has a 7-handicap and plays several times a week. As usually happens, we traded golf stories and I was surprised to discover he hadn't heard the oldie about the golf-playing gorilla.

I am almost embarrassed to repeat it here. Anyway, it seems that a golf-playing gorilla was brought out to the local country club to test his skill in an actual game. The first hole, a par-5, was 550 yards. The gorilla hit his drive straight down the middle—285 yards. His fairway shot was good for 265 yards and rolled to within 20 feet of the cup. The gorilla's putt was a beauty—260 yards before it even hit the ground.

My friend didn't laugh. His mouth dropped open and he stared off into the distance like a character in a comic strip just before an electric bulb lights up over his head indicating he has just been hit with a hot idea.

"What is it?" I asked.

"That story is not as farfetched as you might think," he said. "Why shouldn't a gorilla be able to play golf? I'm going to talk to my trainer right away. If we can bring this off, it will be the greatest gorilla act of all time. We'll make history."

He pledged me to secrecy because he wanted the Royal Copenhagen Zoo to be the first to boast of a golf-playing gorilla.

His trainer fell in with the idea. They worked with the brightest young gorilla in the primate house. They started with a shortened polo mallet and an oversized softball. Then gradually they lengthened the club, reducing the size of both the clubhead and the ball.

For the first month or so the gorilla would lunge wildly at the ball, like a drunk swinging a broom at a bumblebee. But, little by little, the trainer was able to get the gorilla to shorten his swing. After about four months of steady work, the gorilla developed a fairly controlled swing, although he had a marked tendency to sway.

Then after another three months of daily training, the gorilla showed surprising progress. He learned to keep from swaying and to keep his head still. The best club-weight for the gorilla was an H6—or about twice the head-weight of the average club.

The gorilla finally mastered a short backswing—not quite as short as Doug Sanders's, but short enough. What really excited my friend and the trainer was the gorilla's wrist action. This was something he didn't have to be taught. Those wrists would snap just right as he came into the ball.

It took about a year and a half of solid day-in-and-day-out training before my friend was confident enough to bring the gorilla out to the Royal Deer Park Course. After a few holes my friend couldn't have been more elated. The experiment was working out beautifully. The gorilla, dressed in Gene Sarazen knickers and an orange-striped blazer, quickly demonstrated his aptitude. While he didn't get the fantastic distance of the gorilla in the story, he did manage to hit about 190–200 yards. The shots were occasionally erratic but no more so than those of the average bogey player.

The fairway shots tended to be more troublesome than the others. Not having the ball teed up was a problem. Sometimes the gorilla would top the ball and just about shear off a piece of it. And the divots, when he hit under the ball, were not to be believed—huge clumps of earth the size of one of Pearl Bailey's wigs and weighing about two pounds. But the clubhead made contact with the ball just the same.

What was truly astounding was that, unlike the gorilla in the story, the Copenhagen gorilla had no difficulty with his putting. In fact, this was the best part of his game. He had the advantage of being able to lie flat on his stomach behind the ball in lining up the pathway to the cup. He had a good sense of distance and knew how to make allowances for the varying conditions of different greens. Unlike most players, the gorilla was not psyched out once he took a putter in his hands. In the first full game he played he had only two three-putt greens on the round.

My friend toted up the score at the end of 18 holes—103 strokes, not bad considering it was the gorilla's first time out.

Subsequently, they were able to knock about 10 strokes off the gorilla's score by improving his fairway game.

My friend had succeeded. The number of visitors to

the Royal Copenhagen Zoo increased by 60 percent. The gorilla's act was very simple. Instead of using expensive golf balls, the trainer had the gorilla hit Ping-Pong balls directly at the delighted audience. Then the gorilla would put on a demonstration of putting. The floor was covered with an Astroturf circular carpet about 25 feet in diameter. The crowds would go wild with enthusiasm when the gorilla dropped putts of 12 feet or more.

I wish I could say that this report has a happy ending. Unfortunately, neither my friend nor the trainer was able to anticipate the unusual turn their experiment was to take. They hadn't counted on the fact that the gorilla, having learned the game, would insist on playing almost every day. If he wasn't taken out to the Royal Deer Park Golf Course, he would refuse to eat and would moan most of the day. And even when they allowed him to play, he wasn't satisfied with 18 holes. He insisted on going on and would put up a terrible struggle when they tried to lead him back to the zoo's truck. He had to be tranquilized by injection just to get the golf club out of his hands.

Another unexpected development was that the gorilla became morose because his mate wasn't allowed to go with him to the golf course. Finally, it became necessary for the trainer to teach golf to the female gorilla, too. The female had her own ideas about the purpose of the game. The only part of golf that really seemed to appeal to her was making mammoth divots. She didn't even need the pretext of a golf ball on the fairway to launch an attack on the turf. She would hack away at will, letting out shrieks of joy with each clump of earth that spurted into the air.

I must not neglect to mention the fact that the gorillas had atrocious golf manners. They had a possessive feeling about the sport and resented humans using what they believed to be their own private playground. If there were golfers on the fairway in front of them, the gorillas had to be restrained from taking off after the players, brandishing their clubs to the accompaniment of savage shrieks.

Naturally, this was very disconcerting to the players, especially to those who were on the Royal Deer Park Course for the first time and unaware of the golf-playing gorillas (I could imagine how the players must have felt—sizing up their fairway shots and settling over their ball, only to hear terrifying cries and then looking up at two gorillas bearing down on them flailing golf clubs).

The addiction of the gorillas to golf made them almost suicidal if they missed a single day on the links. To cap it all, the female gorilla became pregnant. X-ray examination showed she was going to have twins. The zoo director and the trainer had a serious talk at this point. They could foresee what would happen. The parent gorillas would insist that their young go with them and play, too. It was bad enough the way it was, with the fairways being chewed up, two groundskeepers resigning, and members of the club complaining about having to allow gorillas to play through. But a whole new generation of gorillas coming along was more than anyone could take.

The outcome was inevitable. The gorillas had to be shipped away to the government wildlife park in Kenya. It was a sad day—not just for the gorillas but for my friend and the trainer—when the creatures were loaded onto the truck. My friend could tell from the gorilla's eyes that the animal, who had been crying for a long time, knew that something terrible was about to happen. So my friend got both bags of golf clubs and put them in the packing cage.

Then, when the gorillas were tranquilized and loaded into the cage, my friend went up to them for his last look.

The gorillas were huddled in opposite corners, each clinging to a bag of golf clubs.

My friend is not given to sentimentality, but he told me it was one of the most poignant scenes he had ever witnessed. And he felt guilty for having been responsible for the chain of events that had led to such a melancholy ending.

I told my friend that his feelings of guilt were nothing compared to my own, for I was the one who got him started.

What happened to the gorillas after they arrived in Kenya? My friend says that they were allowed to keep the clubs, and they used up, in a couple of months, the four dozen balls stuffed into the pockets of the golf bag. Thereafter, the gorillas would swing at pieces of dried dung that abounded in the wildlife park, or they would hack away at the grasslands, making divots even larger than the ones that caused so much grief in Copenhagen.

This completes the story except for a brief footnote. During the three months before the gorillas left Copenhagen, a team of zoologists and anthropologists carefully studied the creatures. The proficiency of the gorillas in golf—the male, at least, scored consistently in the low 90s—could not be explained by anything known in science about the remarkable learning skills of gorillas or about the advanced teaching techniques of gorilla training. The more the academicians observed films of the male gorilla playing golf, the more convinced they were that they were dealing with atavistic phenomena.

Their reluctant and final conclusion was that golf was a natural and almost instinctive activity with gorillas, a form of recreation that in one form or another was native to their distant ancestors.

The corollary, of course, is that the human species, in supporting the game, is actually engaging in a form of early ancestral worship.

What the scholars are saying, in effect, is that the gorillas didn't get golf from man but that man got golf from gorillas. Fortunately, the scholars can't prove it. Just the same, I get a sinking feeling every time I think about it.

HOW I TAUGHT GOLDA MEIR
TO PLAY GOLF—ALMOST

This is mostly about my experiences as special golf instructor to Prime Minister Golda Meir of Israel. But the beginning of this story concerns Ben-Gurion.

In 1958, when I first became involved in the Israeli golf scene, Ben-Gurion was the Israeli prime minister. Some of Ben-Gurion's foreign policy advisers were under the impression that Israel was at a disadvantage in its dealings with the United States because it lacked golf capability. Eisenhower was then president of the United States. He liked to bring his eminent guests to Camp David where the official proceedings would be interrupted at least once a day for a round of golf. Some of the most fruitful discussions were held in a golf cart or in the clubhouse.

The clinching argument for Ben-Gurion was that a photograph of him playing golf with Ike would confer great prestige on Israel in the community of nations—almost as though Israel were able to announce that it had developed its own Trident submarine and Polaris missile. Ben-Gurion was then in his seventies but in good physical condition. Those closest to him felt he should have no difficulty in mastering the game—at least to the extent of being able to play with Ike, who was then shooting in the mid-90s.

Ben-Gurion was also told that it would be in Israel's national interest to build a golf course—not just as an international status symbol but as a tourist attraction. Israel was putting millions of dollars each year into tourist advertising but kept bumping into complaints from travel agents who said their customers might be more interested in visiting biblical sites if they were adjacent to a golf course.

It was at this point that my own involvement began. I received a telephone call asking me to come to Israel both for the purpose of teaching Ben-Gurion how to play and to help design an 18-hole course. I shall never forget my first meeting with the venerable Israeli leader. He had a large shaggy head, into which were set small eyes that struck sparks every time they twinkled. He was blunt and hearty and said he thought taking up golf was a lot of foolishness but that he would do anything to improve Israel's trade balance. My first job, he said, was to help design a golf course, for which the government would provide land at Caesarea, famous site of the old Roman ruins. He wanted me to take as much time as required. Then I would return to Jerusalem to give him golf lessons, which would be top secret until he was ready to be put on public exhibition.

Four months later, having fulfilled my mission in Caesarea, I set about the second and more consequential part of my assignment—teaching golf to a seventy-three-year-old man who never before had even touched a golf club. My first five sessions with Ben-Gurion were unforgettable. He discoursed on history, philosophy, anthropology, astronomy, biology, zoology, and architecture. He was the most energetic storyteller I ever met. One way or another he contrived, week after week, to defer his golf lessons.

Finally, he let the cat out of the bag. He took me into his inner office, shut the door securely, turned off the phones, sat me down on the couch reserved for visitors of state, and shared his big secret.

He had never intended, he said, to go all the way. He had agreed to the scheme because of something he alone knew. He had made up his mind six months earlier that he was going to resign at an appropriate time—certainly no later than the spring of 1959. Therefore there would be no point in his learning to play.

I asked the obvious question: Why, then, did he agree to the scheme in the first place?

He threw back that beautiful shaggy head, then his face broke wide open into the most appealing grin I had seen since I first saw a picture of Will Rogers.

"Simple," he said. "I knew that my successor would be Golda Meir. I wanted to create a precedent that would be binding on her. I would be involved in this project just long enough to commit my successor as well. And every time I think of Golda playing golf, it makes me feel good all over. It isn't easy to feel good these days. Do you blame me?"

"What makes you think she'll do it?" I asked.

"She would have no way of refusing—not when all the advisers go to work on her the way they did on me. It might not even be necessary to bring in the advisers. I think I can do it all by myself."

He squinted at his watch.

"It is now ten forty-five A.M. I telephoned her yesterday and asked her to come to my office at eleven. I want her to meet you, just so she'll know how serious I am."

I was staggered by this sudden turn of events. Like Ben-Gurion, I could think of nothing more implausible than Golda Meir on a golf course. She had never impressed me as anyone who could have anything on her mind other than the security and stability of Israel. I was afraid she would boot me right onto the next plane to the U.S.A.—and I told Ben-Gurion so.

"You're absolutely wrong," he said calmly. "Just watch me go to work on her."

A few minutes later, Mrs. Meir arrived at the prime minister's office. Her greeting was brief, almost curt.

Ben-Gurion's anticipations were eerily correct. In a matter-of-fact way, he told Golda that he was taking her into his confidence, and that the only other person who knew what he was about to say was myself. He said he intended, at the end of the month, to announce his retirement and that he would throw all his weight behind her as his successor.

For maybe an hour they discussed the problems of government and the obvious need to make the transition as smoothly as possible. Then, without the slightest change of inflection in his voice or expression, he said he had accepted the advice of the top people in the government about the considerable advantage to Israel of a prime minister who could play golf with the American president if need be. And that was why they had brought me to Israel.

Then he sat back in his seat and, with a straight face, waited for the message to sink in. Mrs. Meir wasn't fazed.

"That makes good sense," she said after only a few seconds. Then, looking squarely at me, she asked without the slightest sign of any incredulity: "When do we start?"

Ben-Gurion couldn't conceal his delight.

"See," he exclaimed, "I told you Golda would do anything for Israel. She'll make a superb student!"

If by "superb" Ben-Gurion was thinking of her willingness to learn everything possible about the game, he was entirely correct. But if he meant that it would be an easy job for me, he was as wide of the mark as if he had described Arafat as a debonair ballroom dancer.

An easy student she was not.

At our first session, she said she didn't want to do anything except hear me discourse on the theory and practice of golf. This I did for about ninety minutes, describing the dynamics of the golf swing and drawing little sketches to show her the different elements involved in hitting the ball accurately and in a way that was smooth and graceful.

She took notes and said that she would prefer to have another skull session or two before working with the clubs.

At our third session, she asked questions.

"Why do you say you want me to concentrate on keeping a firm left arm, using the right arm just to steer the club?"

"Because experiences going back over many years by the world's best golfers have demonstrated that the firm left arm is the best way to transmit power to the ball and keep it from veering off line," I said.

"In that case," she countered, "I could get more power by playing with left-handed clubs, and hitting the ball with a firm right arm from the right side. Since I am right-handed, I am bound to hit more accurately that way and I could probably hit it farther, too."

I made the mistake of trying to refute the argument before thinking it through by saying that it was unnatural for a right-handed player to hit the ball with the left side of his body farthest away from the green.

"Nonsense!" she said. "It's no more unnatural than a right-handed tennis player turning to his left when hitting a backhand shot."

As I thought about it, I knew she had all the logic on her side, so I decided to simplify the argument.

"Very well," I said, "we will have two sets of clubs, one lefty, the other righty. I think you will find that using the right-handed clubs will be much easier."

"I don't think so," she replied. "There's no point in being extravagant. One set of clubs is enough. And if we start the correct way—that is, using clubs that I can hit with my right arm—then we'll develop good habits all the way."

At our next talk session, she asked if I still believed that the right way to hit the golf ball was by concentrating on a firm left arm and allowing the right arm to keep the club in line.

I said yes.

"Well, then," she said, "how do you account for the fact that Tommy Armour and Gene Sarazen say that the right arm is the power arm? I've had my assistants do some research on the golf swing and they've gone through all the best books on the subject and some of your best American golfers disagree with you. What do you think of Gene Sarazen?"

"A great golfer," I said.

"Well, here he says that the left arm should be the steering arm and the right arm is the one that you should feel hitting the ball."

"I still think it would be better for a beginning player to concentrate on a straight left arm," I said, somewhat weakly. "Then, after a few years, you can begin to feed in the controlled power from your right arm."

"All right," she said, "then why did Gene Sarazen address his advice to beginners? Did you remember to order the left-handed clubs?"

I said the left-handed clubs would arrive in a few days.

"Very good," she said. "Now, what did you mean when you said that I had to concentrate on swinging slowly?"

"Just that there was no direct connection between a fast swing and the distance traveled by the ball," I replied.

"How can you say that," she asked, "when Arnold Palmer says in this book right on the top of my desk that you've really got to take a good cut at the ball, as he puts it?"

"Well," I said, "the professional players have been able to groove a pretty fast swing and they know how to control it."

"But that's not what you said earlier," she said abruptly. "You said there's no connection between a fast swing and distance."

"That's still correct," I said. "The important thing is the power that's transmitted to the ball at the instant of impact. That means that legs, hips, shoulders, and arms all have to be synchronized in a power flow to the ball."

"So a fast swing is not necessary?"

"No."

"Then, why are the American professionals turning to lighter clubs? My assistant underlined an article for me that said that Jack Nicklaus was using very light clubs because he could generate more clubhead speed."

I pointed out that what was good for Jack Nicklaus wasn't necessarily good for beginning players.

"Oh, so you think I should use heavy clubs?" she asked.

"No, no," I said. "You should use light clubs."

"But you just said that I shouldn't try to imitate the professionals. If light clubs are good for professionals like Nicklaus so they can swing faster, the heavy clubs should be good for beginners like me. Do you think I would swing more slowly with a heavy club than a light club?"

"Yes," I replied, "but it probably would be more difficult to manage and you might hit wilder shots."

"But you just said that I would hit wild shots if I swung faster, and this is what happens when you use lighter clubs, according to Mr. Nicklaus."

I was beginning to get a little weary. "What I mean is," I said, "I want you to use very light clubs so that you can handle them more easily than heavier clubs."

"You haven't seen me handle any clubs. What makes you say I can't handle the heavier club?"

I decided to concede that particular point. "All I'm trying to say is that just because a professional player does things a certain way doesn't mean it's good for everyone. For example, the pros use clubs with stiff shafts. The average player uses a club with a whippy shaft."

"Why is that?"

"The whippy shaft gives the average player more distance. The stiff shaft provides more accuracy. The professional player gets plenty of distance and wants the additional accuracy."

"Forgive me, Mr. Shitewell," she said, "but I find it difficult to follow your logic."

Like most mortals, I don't like having my name mispronounced.

"The name is Sitewell," I said. "Please tell me what is so illogical about what I just said."

"What would you say is the greatest problem of the average player?" she asked. "Accuracy or distance?"

"Accuracy, of course."

"Then why shouldn't the average player use a stiff shaft for accuracy, and leave the whippy club to the professional player who ought to know how to hit a ball straight and who can probably use the extra distance? Haven't you got this whole thing turned around?"

I could feel a rush of blood to the head. There was nothing I could say that wasn't being challenged. I could just imagine what would happen to my standing as a teacher when Golda Meir began playing golf with left-handed clubs and stiff shafts.

"I know it may sound very illogical, but the game of golf has been going on a long time and some things have proven out by trial and error," I said.

"Like whippy shafts that increase the likelihood of error for beginners or average players, and stiff shafts for professionals?"

"Strange as it may seem, yes."

"Or like hitting with your weaker arm, the left one, to get more power?"

"Yes," I said lamely.

"You make it seem that the great players all agree."

"On the fundamentals, certainly."

"The most fundamental thing of all in golf is swing—correct?"

"Correct," I said.

"They why do the very best players swing differently? I had some of my assistants do research on this. Would you say that Arnold Palmer is a good player?"

"Of course."

"And Jack Nicklaus?"

"Ditto."

"And Miller Barber, Billy Casper, and Lee Trevino?"

"Triple ditto."

"Then if they agree on the fundamentals, they should certainly agree on the golf swing."

"Well . . ." I knew I was waffling.

"Here are some pictures of all those players at various stages of their golf swings. If they agree on the fundamentals, why do they look so different doing the same thing?"

I was trying to think of an answer, but none came to mind that I thought she would find persuasive.

"Mr. Palmer looks as if he's trying to put a hole in the ceiling when he finishes his swing," she said. "Mr. Nicklaus looks as though he's trying to use the club head to get at an itch deep down his back at the end of his swing. And Mr. Trevino swings as though he's trying to yank a sled out of a ditch."

I was beginning to feel relieved that I hadn't been sent to Israel to negotiate a treaty with Mrs. Meir. I decided to run up the white flag.

"Mrs. Meir," I said. "You are absolutely right. There are many ways to hit a golf ball correctly. What I propose to do is to help you find a way to hit a golf ball that is right for you."

"Then you agree I should play with heavy left-handed clubs and a stiff shaft?"

"We'll give everything a try and if you do better with those clubs, then those are the ones you will use."

I knew my troubles were only beginning.

"One other thing," she said.

"Yes?"

Changing her tone to one of friendly concern, she asked, "Do you happen to know Arnold Palmer?"

"I'm not one of his intimate friends, but I know him fairly well."

"Enough to give him some useful advice and a present from me?"

"What advice? What present?"

"I think he should wear suspenders. Is there any rule that says a golfer shouldn't wear suspenders?"

"Certainly not. Why do you want Arnold Palmer to wear suspenders?"

"So he can concentrate on his game instead of worrying about his pants falling down. My research assistants tell me he is always hitching up his trousers. Which means he is terribly afraid of an accident happening. So it's very simple. I want to give him a pair of suspenders with the compliments of the State of Israel. It'll do wonders for his game."

I suddenly felt homesick.

"Mrs. Meir," I said, with as much courage as I could summon in my dispirited and depleted condition, "I really think you'll do much better without a teacher. You've thought about this game in far more basic ways than many of those who play at it for a living or who, like me, teach it and write about it. I have no doubt that whatever you do will be original and right for you."

"I would appreciate your resignation in writing," she said. "After all, I acquiesced to the urging of my ministers only because I wanted to do the right thing by my country. But if the person they selected to teach me thinks it is in the best interests of Israel that I give up the game, then I am in the clear, am I not?"

And that was the way it ended. Only when I was in the

plane over the Atlantic did I realize that the new prime minister was a chip off the old Ben-Gurion block. She never had any more intention of going through with the scheme than he did. If anything, she outfoxed the wily old Ben-Gurion by putting herself in a position where she could reluctantly withdraw from the enterprise only because I gave up on it myself, thus relieving her of any charge that she was unwilling to serve her country.

Anyway, the project wasn't a total loss. At least the Israeli Tourist Bureau got a golf course out of it.

I also concluded that Israel might not ascend the heights in golf, but it would never come out second best in any high-level negotiations.

THE GREAT JAPANESE
GOLF PLOT

Thanks to my undercover Japanese contacts, I am in a position to reveal one of the best-kept golf secrets in recent years.

Very briefly:

The Japanese government has been involved in a hush-hush international scheme to use the new knowledge in genetics for its aim to wrest the world's golf championship away from the United States. It will be twenty years before this plan will yield the expected full results, but the Japanese are already twenty-seven months into their plan. By 1996, if the scheme succeeds, Japan will have at least six golfers who will average 67.2 for 18 holes in a season of championship play, almost two strokes better than the average winning scores in the past three decades.

The scheme began to hatch two years ago when articles began appearing in the world's scientific press about "recombinant genetics." In laboratories at Harvard and the University of California at Los Angeles, research scientists reasoned that it was possible to unlock DNA, the element that determines hereditary traits in very simple forms of bacteria. Looking ahead, they could envision both the wondrous and terrifying possibilities resulting from the ability of science to recombine genes in order to create new forms of life.

As might be expected, these possibilities touched off one of the most far-reaching debates in the history of modern science. Obviously, if new forms of bacteria could be devised in the laboratory, then that knowledge could be used to produce new disease germs against which even the most powerful antibiotics would be helpless.

More dangerous still was the possibility, clearly recognized by many eminent scientists, that unscrupulous governments could recombine DNA in order to breed human beings according to certain preconceived ideas.

No wonder a cry went up in the American Congress for legislation that would set limits to genetic manipulation.

Whether this field of research is to be governed by law or self-regulation, one thing is clear: Other governments do not consider themselves bound by American laws or practices. Last fall, I went to Japan in an attempt to find out what Japanese geneticists were up to, and also how the Japanese government proposed to deal with the resultant problems. Being able to read Japanese was helpful in following the scientific journals. The trail led to revelations no less sensational than the Pentagon Papers disclosures during the Nixon administration.

It would be highly unwise and, in any case, too risky

79

for me to reveal how I obtained access to these secret papers. Suffice it to say, I was able to work through a Japanese scientist who is profoundly disturbed by the implications of recombinant DNA research and who places the human interest above the national interest. As a result, I am in a position to quote directly from the government papers, which go under the translated code name of "Project Links" *(Dematsu Chongai).*

The first document, not dissimilar to the famous letter about atomic energy to President Roosevelt from a group of scientists led by Albert Einstein, was sent to the Japanese prime minister on April 9, 1975, by three of Japan's most eminent biologists. They called attention to the new field of recombinant DNA just opening up, and proposed that a secret government commission be appointed that would not only draw up the guidelines for research but would use this knowledge to advance the international position of Japan.

The suggestion was accepted and a commission, appointed in May 1976, has been steadily at work since that date. Three interim reports have been received from the commissioner, one of them with the above code name, *Dematsu Chongai.* I have seen a copy of this report and, quite frankly, because of my dedication to American world leadership in golf, I am alarmed. I have no doubt that our CIA has a copy of the entire report; but what worries me is that I can't think of anything the United States government can do about it.

Very briefly, the scheme calls for the secret "acquisition" of DNA from the germ plasm of ten of America's top golfers. The Japanese have been "breeding" wrestlers and actors for many centuries. Through selective mating and rigorous training, they have been able, for example, to produce human mastodons (Sumo wrestlers) who weight up to 400 pounds. The Japanese have also been able to produce, through techniques used in breeding thoroughbred racing horses and dogs, male actors who have falsetto voices and who can act the parts of women *(Gikamanu Hi-deko)*. The notion, therefore, of "breeding" supergolfers was not without precedent in other Japanese fields. What the new knowledge of genetic engineering offered was a chance to produce champion golfers in a single generation.

On a more practical side, what made this whole project more plausible was the secret discovery that the necessary DNA, through electronic and chemical process, could be extracted from fingernails. Although the Japanese are well advanced in their scientific study of cloning, it is felt that the actual perfection of the cloning process would be some decades away. Their research, however, has developed the process by which the DNA from fingernail specimens can be used to produce the proper genetic properties through normal reproductive processes.

Once the government gave its approval, the project began to move. The first thing that was done, it is clear from these papers, was to define a perfect golfer. It was agreed that a perfect golfer was one who possessed:

1. The concentration of Jack Nicklaus.
2. The general personality of Arnold Palmer, as well as Palmer's confidence to make almost impossible shots.
3. The distance off the tee of Jim Dent combined with the driving accuracy of Tom Weiskopf.
4. The ability of Sam Snead to play out of traps.

5. The skill of Ben Crenshaw in playing out of the rough.
6. The strategical intelligence of Byron Nelson.
7. The ability of Lee Trevino to hit a controlled fade.
8. The artistic use by Tom Watson of his 7-, 8-, and 9-irons.
9. The perseverance and personal health of Gary Player.
10. The ability of Billy Casper to adapt to varying conditions of play.

How would it be possible to combine all these attributes in the breeding of a perfect golfer? I quote now from the report itself:

It is necessary to obtain live fingernail specimens not more than one hour old from these distinguished gentlemen. This is a very delicate matter. The ideal way to do it would be with their consent. For a generous consideration, this might be possible. But such an open transaction would require disclosure of the original purpose, and it is doubtful whether such fine American gentlemen would lend their cooperation to a plan for divesting their nation of its world preeminence in golf. Regrettably, therefore, we must obtain the necessary genetic substance without their knowledge if possible.

It is obvious that this would be more difficult with some of these gentlemen than with others. We recommend, therefore, that an intelligence operation be mounted immediately for the purpose of determining the kind of strategy that should be devised to fit each individual. In general, we see three basic plans:

Plan A. Under this plan we would hold an international golf tournament in Japan, offering substantially higher cash prizes than have ever been given before. We would, of course, pay all expenses plus a guaranteed fee of $15,000 for each of the designated golfers.

We will arrange with the hotel at which these distinguished gentlemen will be staying to inform the American gentlemen, although we are certain they are already very well informed of this fact, that nothing is more conducive to a good night's sleep, especially after the physical and emotional drain of tournament golf play, than the world-famous Japanese massage. The hotel will also inform these gentlemen that, along with the massage, a Japanese manicure is being given with the compliments of the tournament committee.

For those gentlemen who acquiesce to this service, we will of course provide the appropriate masseuses. These young ladies should be drawn from the special division of our central intelligence operations. It is requested that they be young women of extraordinary physical endowments and beauty of face. They should also be experts in the artistic as well as the functional attributes of Japanese massage and, of course, manicuring. Special vacuum-sealed receptacles can be devised for preserving and transporting the DNA substance produced by these gentlemen. Once these receptacles reach the laboratory, our scientists can proceed with their electronic equipment to make the essential DNA separation for later recombining with the DNA from the other specimens of the American gentlemen.

Plan B. Some of the golfers on our list may not wish to come to Japan, even with the extraordinary cash inducements they will be offered. In this case, we must be prepared to pursue our project inside the United States. Our intelligence agents will inform us about the distinguished American golfers who are responsive to young ladies of striking beauty and charm. Perhaps we might be able to borrow several such young women from the appropriate division of the CIA, which is obligated to us for the services and facilities made available to them only last month for a special Tokyo project in which they were interested and which required female Japanese operatives who were naturally endowed in a manner that would enhance their persuasiveness.

Exactly how these female operatives would make contact with the distinguished American gentlemen inside the U.S. calls for special determination in each case. In any event, these operatives would be instructed in the procedure to be followed and in the techniques by which our receptacles must be handled. Our agents must gain possession of these receptacles within an hour of the nails being clipped.

Plan C. We must take into account that some of these distinguished gentlemen, for reasons that are not relevant to our purpose, will turn away from the opportunities made available in Plan A and Plan B. It is expected that most of those in this category will have wives and be of little mind to turn elsewhere. Remote though this possibility may seem, it has to be considered.

In such cases, it is proposed that the wives

themselves be secretly approached. They should be told that a project is under way to make germ plasm belonging to the finest specimens of American manhood available for long-term scientific study. The wives should also be told that the men themselves cannot be informed about this project since such knowledge might cause them to bite their nails and that the project requires as much normalization as possible. The wives should be offered $25,000 in cash for their cooperation in serving the purposes of scientific research. Those who agree should be instructed in the use of our special receptacles. They must consent to have our agents pick up these receptacles within an hour.

It is the opinion of this scientific body that, once the receptacles containing the necessary germ plasm of the distinguished American gentlemen are delivered into the care of our leading geneticists, it will be possible to produce a full new DNA set of recombinant genes containing most if not all of the desirable features that have been characteristic of these distinguished American gentlemen.

The Japanese women who will be impregnated with the recombinant germ plasm have already been selected. They are all married. The appropriate arrangements have been made with them and their husbands. Since genetic engineering is capable of ensuring that the children will be largely Japanese in appearance, there should be no problems on that score.

The text above covers the main points of the report by the Japanese scientific commission. The report itself is perhaps twelve times as long as the material quoted, but it consists largely of scientific material not of prime interest to laymen.

How far has the project proceeded? I am informed that, since the project was approved two years ago, the Japanese have been successful in obtaining the required DNA substances from at least six of the golfers named on the original list of ten. I understand further that attempts are going forward to use whatever means are necessary to obtain the vital substance from the remaining four.

It is also my information that, without waiting for the entire ten, the Japanese geneticists have proceeded to recombine the genes of the six American golfers, and the resultant combined germ plasm has led to at least four successful pregnancies and births. The geneticists claim to have every confidence that the four athletes produced by this genetic programming should be able to average less than 69 per round over a season's play. This is somewhat higher than the original goal but good enough to put Japan on a par with the U.S. in world golf.

The Japanese are fairly confident that they will succeed in obtaining the germ plasm of the remaining four American golfers within the next year or two. This means that, around the turn of the century, a second crop of Japanese superstar golfers can be expected to appear on the world scene, bringing with them the startling capability of a 67.2 average for a season's play. This will clearly reinforce the dominance of Japan.

Can anything be done?

The most obvious thing to be done is for us to borrow a leaf from the Japanese. There is no reason why we cannot use recombinant DNA to stay ahead, or at least stay even. Since American geneticists ought to be able to obtain the full cooperation of our outstanding golfers and not have to resort to complicated undercover schemes, there ought to be no difficulty in obtaining the DNA that could produce a breed of American golfers with—hold your hat—a 66.5 scoring capability over a season's play.

Failing this, we ought to assign our scientists to a project that would devise a test for determining whether the DNA of any tournament golfer (or any athlete, for that matter) shows evidence of genetic engineering. Those golfers can be disqualified. One way or another, the supremacy of American golf must be assured.

THE WORST PLAYED HOLE
IN THE HISTORY OF GOLF

Ask the average golfer about the worst hole of golf ever played, and he will have little difficulty in responding, drawing upon his vast store of personal experiences, without identifying himself as a participant. Such an exercise of the memory can be useful. Sometimes the best way to improve one's game is to know all the things that have gone wrong before. Santayana, the famous philosopher, no doubt had golf in mind when he said that the only sure way to contribute to the advance of civilization is to memorize its failures.

I have my own nomination for the worst single hole of golf ever played: It happened on February 5, 1965, on the 5th hole of the famous Puerto Rico Dorado Beach golf playground. The golfer responsible for the record was Cleveland Amory, writer, social historian, humorist, and animal benefactor. The 5th hole at the East course is a par-5 dogleg, with a lake on the left flanking the fairway, and a pond in front of a sharply elevated green.

Amory is a long-ball hitter. He has an unorthodox

stance—feet far apart with his weight so far forward that the gravitational problem is disconcerting to terrified observers. Breaking the dogleg across the water and positioning the ball for a birdie attempt calls for a drive of about 270 yards—well within Amory's capability. Amory's drive was long enough but was too far to the left, plopping in the water about 30 yards from shore.

On the second tee attempt, Amory lost his balance and broke his club when it rammed into the ground. He picked himself up, grinned, and announced that it was just a practice swing. The interpretation was of course disallowed by the other players, including his partner (myself).

Lying 5, he now teed up again with a borrowed club. His drive was one of the longest he had ever hit in his life, coming to rest just at the water's edge. I doubted that it was playable. Rather than take a penalty and drop the ball on high ground, however, Amory decided to play the ball as it lay. He removed his shoes and socks, rolled up his trousers, and positioned himself in the water. There was one thing, however, he didn't take into account. His own bulk (he is 6 foot 4 inches and weighs at least 260) caused the water level of the lake to rise just enough to put a thin film of water over the ball.

This natural event served only to fortify Amory's resolve. He switched from a 4-iron to a 6-iron in order to get the benefit of additional loft. He was 180 yards from the elevated green, which added the equivalent of 30 yards to the distance. But he was capable of getting that much distance out of a 6-iron, if he hit it hard enough. So he widened his stance and dug in with his heels, not taking into account the extreme softness of the subsurface turf. As he started his swing, his feet sank into the mud. Since this reduced the mobility of the lower part of his torso, he tried to compensate by additional arm velocity on the downswing. But he didn't allow sufficiently for the fact that his feet were well below the level of the ball. The result was that the clubhead plunged deep into the soft ground behind the ball, causing the ball to pop into the air a few inches and then settle back in the water. In the attempt to yank the bent club out of the mud, Amory lost his balance and fell backward into the water.

Amory's fortitude and determination were never more in evidence than at this juncture. He rose from the water with surprising grace for one of his bulk and announced his intention to go on with the game. He raised the damaged club in a gesture of defiance. Then, in an act of uncharacteristic prudence, he took a low iron from his bag for a punch shot to dry land. The shot was perfectly executed.

At this point, the tally was seven strokes, not to mention two ruined clubs. Amory's eighth shot was a beauty—a controlled 5-iron 170 yards straight to the pin. In fact, it hit the pin, caroming back in a straight line and catching the slope running down to the pond in front of the green.

I was almost afraid to look at Amory. After all that happened, he was entitled to at least one good break. But it was not to be. He stood riveted to the spot where he had hit the ball, watching it balefully as it picked up speed down the hill, finally plopping into the pond, too deep to play even for a man of his intrepid disposition.

None of us would have blamed Amory if he had decided at this point to call it a day. But adversity, especially on a golf course, has a way of supplying people with ever-higher levels of resolve. Very carefully, Amory picked his way down the slippery bank, overgrown with thorny brush. He was wearing shorts, so his legs had little protection against nature's needles. The ball was too deep in the water for a shot; Amory fished it out and then skirted the shore to the far side of the pond to the drop area. The ball had a favorable lie; Amory hit it with a wedge. The shot was straight but a trifle strong and the ball trickled into the sand trap just beyond the green where it nestled into a footprint.

Unfortunately, Amory's first trap shot buried itself under the lip. He was prepared to pop it out with a hooded sand wedge when the golf marshal arrived on the scene in an electric cart. He said that five foursomes were now bunched up. He suggested we either pick up and go on to the next hole or let them through.

It was at this point that Amory's steam valve broke. All the frustration and wrath that had been building up were now turned on the marshal. Did the marshal suppose he was talking to a dub, Amory demanded. Didn't the marshal realize that Amory had been the captain of the Harvard golf team? The most important convention in golf, he informed the marshal, was the law of reasonable play. Under this law, certain allowances are made for unusual events. One never—repeat, never—asks a competent group of golfers to step aside just because of a few mis-hits on a single hole. Finally, Amory told the marshal to mind his manners lest he, Amory, be impelled to report his lapse to any one of the Rockefeller brothers, owners of the resort, all of whom he knew.

Clearly, the marshal was overmatched. He didn't apologize or anything like that, but he mumbled something to the effect that he was only doing his job. He got back in his electric cart and drove away as fast as possible,

not even bothering to inform the bunched-up players behind us about the disposition of the encounter.

Amory took his victory over the marshal as a matter
of course, then resumed his efforts to get out of the trap,
which he did eventually, but not without adding three
more strokes to his score and a bent shaft on the sand
wedge, the result of a powerful swing that caught the hard
lip of the trap. He 3-putted from a distance of about 12
feet, not bad considering the momentum of poor shots
behind him.

I toted up the score. He was 17 in the hole. There
were also the three wrecked clubs. Dorado Beach had
never seen anything like it. The physical and psychologi-
cal wreckage of what we had just been through was not
beyond description but it was certainly close to being
beyond human endurance.

Yet fate is redemptive. On the very next hole, a par
3 of 187 yards, Amory hit a 4-iron stiff to the pin, then
tapped in for a birdie. As might be expected, this particular hole was the topic of conversation in the locker
room and at the dinner table. Nothing was said about
the 5th hole. In fact, I have since heard Amory refer to
his birdie at number 6 a number of times, but never to
its predecessor.

PERSONALS

MANUFACTURER'S OVERRUN
of Napoleon statues. Life-
size, can be used as scare-
crows, burglar foils, or
supports for sagging
entablatures. Sturdy
unbreakable plastic in
mauve or Prussian blue;
stern expression. SR/W
Box TE.

WILL THE PARTY who spilled beer all over the upholstery of my unlocked new Cadillac at Madison Avenue and 51st Street, N.Y.C., on Sunday, January 6 please tell me what the joke was all about. SR/W Box QZ.

OUR COMPUTERIZED telephone answering service is scientifically calibrated to judge human personality just by voice vibrations and tonal quality. We can detect within 10 seconds whether the person who wishes to speak to you is trying to borrow money or sell you worthless merchandise. Write for information. Electronic Voice Analysis. SR/W Box SE.

PHILADELPHIANS are superior intellectually, socially, biologically. Proof available on request. New Yorkers need not apply. SR/W Box MT.

5

K. Jason Sitewell
as Lexicographer
and Biographer

K.J.S. proved himself to be more than a scholarly analyst of the perils of golf. He was a student of punctuation and undertook original research into the origin of the period. Leaving no stone unturned in his assault on the written word, he also turned to biography, of which the second article in this chapter—the saga of Poop Glover—is a sample.

THE INVENTOR OF THE PERIOD

Soon there will occur an event of profound importance to the literatures of all languages. I refer to the 2,500th birthday of Kohmar Pehriad (544–493 B.C.), inventor of punctuation in written language. He also figures prominently in the development of copyright law, which I shall discuss in a moment. Pehriad was the leading literary figure of Macedonia in the pre-Christian era. His writings ranged from poetry to speculations on astronomy and physics. Few of these writings remain. What does remain, however, is his successful reform of written language in virtually all tongues.

In those days written language was continuous. There were no sentence or paragraph breaks. Pehriad's own writings represent the first recorded use of the small round dot to indicate the end of a completed unit of expression. More important than that is the fact that he gave thirty years of his life, traveling throughout ancient Greece, Rome, Persia, North Africa, and Asia, in the effort to obtain local acceptance of the small dot that has since done so much for literature.

His first great success outside his country came when he was able to persuade some Greek scholars to issue a complete version of Homer's *Odyssey* and *Iliad,* with the small round dots in the proper places. Up to that time Homer had had a limited following in Greece. With the reformed version, however, his work gained widespread acceptance. Pehriad's next success came in Constantinople, where he was directly responsible for the first manuscript of the Hebrew Torah containing periods.

As he traveled from place to place, the logic of Pehriad's argument became increasingly accepted. It was not necessary, he reasoned, for each language to devise its own mark to denote a proper cause. The small round dot could be used in all languages. The stark simplicity of this idea, amounting virtually to genius, is doubtless responsible for the fact that every written language in the world today uses the small round dot. Thus, Pehriad's contribution is not only to his own country but to mankind.

Pehriad's reward, of course, is that the small round dot has been named after him, our spelling of his name having been anglicized. Even in a country as remote as Nepal, the influence of Pehriad today is to be found in the fact that the sentence dot is called a *pahyed.* In China it is called *pi-yen.* In Malaya, *peeyeed.* In New Guinea the capital *P* is used as a gesture of respect to the inventor in its word, *Peelied.*

Pehriad's efforts did not stop with the period. He was also concerned with the need for an appropriate marking that might correspond to the pause in a person's speech in the middle of an incompleted sentence. This led him to devise what we now know as the comma, also named after him (Kohmar). It is interesting to read in his *Journal* that he later felt he had made a mistake in not using the comma marking instead of the period and vice versa. "The dot with the curved descending tail is the more impressive and visible mark and should therefore have been used for the more important purpose of indicating the end of a sentence," he wrote. "The dot slows up the reader and should therefore have been used to indicate a pause." Pehriad, in his declining years, sought to bring about this shift in comma-period usage, but by this time the custom had hardened.

It remained for Pehriad's son to devise yet other markings for the purpose of strengthening the written language. Apos-Trophe Pehriad felt that the comma was adaptable to a wide variety of purposes, so long as its position could be varied. He used it inside a word to denote the abbreviation; at the end of a word to denote possession; in tandem to denote quotation, with the mark inverted at the beginning of the quotation. As in the case of his father, his invention bears his name.

There is no evidence that the Pehriads, father or son, invented either the question mark or the exclamation point. The younger Pehriad, however, did attempt to indicate emphasis inside a sentence. If the emotion registered in the pronunciation of a word was scorn or anger he placed a concave curve atop the key word to be emphasized. If a person wished to give a sorrowful or sad expression to a word the marking was a convex curve below the word. If a person's speech was staccato or jerky young Pehriad required the writer to put down each word slantwise. One shudders at the difficulties this would have caused printers had the reform been generally adopted.

The historical verdict on young Pehriad must be that, outside of his juggling of commas so that they became apostrophes or quotation marks, he lacked the simple directness and the judgment that made his father the only literary figure in history whose contribution is visible in almost every piece of writing anywhere in the world, except, of course, in the poetry of e. e. cummings and other modern innovators.

But the significance of the Pehriads is not confined to the small round dot or the comma. I wrote at the start that they figured indirectly in the development of copyright law. What happened was that a descendant of Apos-Trophe and of Pehriad moved to Rome, where he became a highly successful counselor-at-law. Pehriad Apullus had proper pride in the family name but had always felt that his ancestors had been inexcusably amateurish and un-businesslike. Apullus set out to earn for himself the tangible rewards that he felt the old folks had overlooked. Under old Roman law direct descendants could obtain legal rights to inventions if their forebears had neglected to take out patents.

Apullus had considerable influence in the Roman courts. He contended that the period was an invention and therefore subject to royalties. To demonstrate his high-mindedness he informed the court that, though he would insist on full right to the period, he would make a gift of the comma to the state. Impressed by the fairness of the man, the court granted him a copyright on the period, and prescribed a fee of one drachma for any piece of writing containing more than 100 periods. Manuscripts containing upward of 500 periods were to bring a flat royalty of ten drachmas. This marked the beginning of the short essay in ancient Rome.

Apullus discreetly waited several years before seeking an extension of his copyright to include any piece of writing, whatever the length and whatever the nature. Even private letters were to be subject to royalty for the use of periods. By this time he had insinuated himself into the circle of those closest to Octavius. Rome was sorely pressed for funds and it was Apullus's ingenious proposal to Octavius that, in addition to extending his royalty to include any use of periods, the government itself should collect a modest tax.

Serious consideration was given to this idea but it was eventually discarded because of the tremendous increase it would require in the number of tax investigators. There was also some apprehension in government quarters that many citizens would circumvent the law by using substitute markings instead of periods.

In any event, during the period of the debate general fear spread through the populace. Suetonius, in his *Lives of the Caesars,* writes that the general citizenry came close to giving up writing altogether for fear that some retroactive law would be passed compelling them to pay both royalty and tax on every period they had ever used in their lifetimes. As might be expected, this led to incredibly involved, nonstop sentences, clear traces of which are still discernible in modern times.

In an attempt to ridicule the proposed law some people exclaimed "Period!" in the proper places during their conversations. This habit has persisted to the present day.

Eventually the situation in ancient Rome was straightened out. In the course of so doing, Roman law devised what Anglo-Saxon law commonly accepts as the basis for copyright. Recognizing that some time limit ought to be set to the benefits Apullus would derive from his copyright, the Roman courts decreed that beyond Apullus's generation no royalties would be paid. A complicating factor, of course, in terms of precedent, involved the original inventor of the period, who had received no rewards for his work. This is what led the Roman courts to decree that the benefits of copyright should be limited to a single generation, or twenty-six years. But the absolute limit was fixed at fifty-two years.

Outside his native Macedonia and, to a lesser extent, Italy, the inventor of the period is not generally recognized. The 2,500th anniversary of his birth (April 1 A.F.D.) gives all of us a long-deferred opportunity to pay homage to a man who has made written language not only intelligible but possible. The period did not come about by accident. Someone had to invent it and fight for it.

THE AMAZING SAGA
OF "POOP" GLOVER

Before I tell you how I tracked down "Poop" Glover, the child chess prodigy, perhaps I ought to review some of the main facts of his young life, even though you probably know the general story.

His real name was Paul, and it was no coincidence, as I later learned, that he had been named after Paul Morphy, the great American chess master a century ago. At the age of three months, Paul became a ward of the Flatbush Home for Orphans in Brooklyn, New York. He didn't learn how to speak until he was five—by which time, amazingly enough, he had already beaten a large number of skilled adult chess players, some of whom were of tournament caliber. It was inevitable that he would be compared with Bobby Fischer, another Brooklyn product, but most chess experts who had played against Poop and Bobby at about the same age said that Poop had the edge. The only word he would utter while playing chess was "poop"—when he wished to announce checkmate. At first, his opponents saw no connection between the word "poop," uttered in laconic and disconnected fashion, and the fact of impending checkmate. The reason they were slow in perceiving the significance of the term was that the child would use it to announce checkmate four or five moves before the coup de grace—in itself a phenomenon. In Brooklyn chess circles, inevitably, he became known as "Poop."

Among the feats accumulated by the young chess master were his performances at the Downtown Brooklyn Chess Club when, at the age of six, still unable to speak except in the crudest sentences, he played eighteen boards simultaneously, winning seventeen and tying one.

The tie game was played against Benny Farber, the Brooklyn champion whose great distinction was that he had beaten Bobby Fischer seven out of eleven times in a series of games when Fischer was nine years old. In head-to-head play between Farber and Glover, played over a three-year period—between the time Poop was five and eight years old—the best Benny Farber could do was to tie six games while losing twenty-three.

Poop was brought to the famed Manhattan Chess Club for the first time when he was seven. He proceeded to astound the Manhattan chess masters by winning all five matches, including a game against the formidable Fairfield Hoban. Hoban, who had twice beaten Sam Reshevsky, had no hesitation in declaring that Glover at seven was the equal of Fischer at fourteen. Cleveland Amory, the social critic and writer, and captain of the Harvard Club chess team, played Poop the week following the child's astonishing performance at the Manhattan Chess Club. The newspapers quoted Amory, who lost three quick games to Glover, as saying he was certain that, long before the child's tenth birthday, Poop would be capable of defeating any chess grand master in the world, Botvinnik, Tal, Spassky, and Fischer not excluded.

In 1967, at the age of twelve, Poop Glover suddenly and inexplicably gave up chess. Since Poop spoke only in monosyllables, no one, not even his guardians at the orphanage, could account for the child's totally unexpected and obstinate refusal to play. It was thought at first that his lack of interest was only temporary. But, with the passing of weeks and months, he showed not the slightest desire to return to the chessboard.

For a long time, in fact, Paul Glover dropped completely out of the news. Having followed him closely, I wondered what had happened. Theoretically, he should be ready to play in major tournaments.

I decided to undertake an informal investigation. My first call was at the Flatbush Home for Orphans. A new director was then in charge. He remembered Paul Glover, to be sure, but said that the boy had been adopted by a family in Indiana. I was allowed to consult the orphanage records and ascertained that a retired child psychologist and his wife had appeared one day at the orphanage and presented evidence showing that they had some kinship to the woman who was believed to have been Poop's mother. When the elderly couple met Poop for the first time, the child was friendly and responsive. With the concurrence of orphanage officials, the legal formalities of adoption were quickly fulfilled. The child rather matter-of-factly accepted his new situation, much in the manner of an unemotional stockbroker discounting future changes in the fortunes of a stock.

Sensing a good story, I flew out to Indianapolis, rented a car, and drove to Elkhart, where I located the home of the retired child psychologist. A boy whom I guessed to be Poop was mowing the ample sloping lawn in front of a rather commodious ranch-style house set well back from the road on an acre-or-more plot.

The boy scarcely looked up at me as I passed him on my way up the path to the front door. The professor's wife answered the chimes set off by my ring. She was an affable, attractive woman. I told her I had come from New Rochelle, New York, and that I hoped I might talk to her and her husband about their adopted son. She seemed not at all jarred by this information; she smiled and invited me into the house. She took my coat and led me into the library, where she asked me to make myself comfortable while she fetched the professor.

I scanned the professor's book collection. There were

at least a thousand volumes on psychology and philosophy. The titles on child psychology alone filled five wide shelves. I took down four or five books and saw that the margins and end papers were filled with penciled notes, written in a neat hand. I recalled having read an article by Mortimer Adler, perhaps in the *Saturday Review* two decades ago, scorning the notion that books should be kept in pristine condition. The best thing that could happen to a book, Adler wrote, was to give evidence of having set ideas in motion. In this sense, the professor's books were practically jumping. Adler would have been delighted.

While I was thus engaged, the professor and his wife entered the study. I was somewhat startled when I saw his resemblance to the late John Dewey, whom I had known at Teachers College of Columbia University.

"You wanted to see me?" he asked.

I apologized for the intrusion, then explained I was a freelance writer and had helped a few nationally known chess players in writing books about the game.

While his wife served coffee, the professor asked me about my interest in their adopted child.

I knew the only approach to such a man was the unvarnished one. I told him I wanted to find out why the boy had given up the game—and why the professor and his wife had adopted him. I thought it might be a good idea to track the story down.

"Yes, of course," said the professor. "It is as much in my interest to talk to you as it is for you to talk to me."

This was a surprise. I had anticipated that I would have to dig hard for my information, yet here was the professor apparently eager to communicate.

"There are, as you might expect," the professor continued, "several conditions to my willingness to tell you the full story. At the moment, I will mention just the first condition—and that is that you do not use my real name in anything you may write. Later, I will tell you the other conditions."

The first condition seemed to me somewhat unrealistic and I said so. After all, if I had been able to find my way to the professor, so would others. Even if I didn't use his real name, people could identify him simply by consulting the records of the orphanage.

"It might not be as easy as all that," he said, looking at me with that same direct, intent gaze I had always associated with Dewey. "The orphanage people telephoned me just after you had gone through their records. The director realized he had probably erred in telling you as much as he did. I told him not to worry about it but requested that he reject any further requests for information."

"Then you expected my visit?"

"We did expect to hear from you, one way or the other. In fact, I did a little research and decided I could trust you."

"Trust me to do what?" I asked. "After all, part of the story is already public domain."

"True, but if I tell you why I don't want to be identified, I think you will understand the reason for my request."

"Fair enough," I said.

"Let's go back to 1959, the year Paul was born. He was named after Paul Morphy, as you may know. Morphy may or may not have been the greatest chess player of his time. What we do know is that he was a romantic figure, was tubercular, wrote poetry, and lived in the heart of the

Latin Quarter in a house that has since become one of the classic architectural landmarks of New Orleans. My great-grandparents were neighbors of Morphy's. Morphy was a sort of Proustian character. He lived a secluded life, kept his shades drawn, emerging infrequently for chess tournaments or for midnight meals in some of the lesser-known all-night cafés in the Quarter. He was bedded down frequently by recurrent attacks of fever and debility—another reason for seclusion.

"My great-grandmother would bring him food and medication. There is reason to believe Morphy was in love with my great-grandmother, and that they were intimate. She was young and raven-haired and had an exquisite olive complexion. She was regarded as one of the most spectacularly beautiful women of New Orleans. At the time of which I speak she was in her late twenties. On a number of occasions, when Morphy was abed with fever, she would stay with him for many hours at a time. My great-grandfather went off to fight in the Civil War and was killed several months later, shortly before his young wife gave birth to a boy. That boy grew up to be a great doctor and surgeon in New Orleans. He was my grandfather. He was also a genius at chess but played in very few tournaments, in which he performed superbly. But his career was medicine. He knew that a dual career was impossible; chess to be played on the tournament level, as you know, calls for a mind that is focused on almost nothing else.

"Yes, I know what you are thinking. You are thinking that my grandfather was the son of Paul Morphy. A natural and inevitable speculation. May I say there is no doubt in my mind that this is so. Some letters found in my great-grandmother's room after her death leave little doubt that her second son was indeed the son of the man who was perhaps the greatest American chess player who ever lived, Lasker and Fischer not excepted. It is significant that my great-grandmother named her son Paul. It was a rather blatant thing for her to do, but that was the way she was, I guess.

"As I said, Paul grew up to be a great doctor. His first son—that would be my own father—was named Paul, Jr. His middle initial was *M*—for Morphy, of course. I know this is complicated; I am sorry. My brother's daughter, like her great-great-grandmother, was left widowed during a war—in this case, the Korean War. This girl, if you can follow the genealogy, was my niece. She left her home in Baton Rouge to come to New York for the purpose—I later learned—of giving secret birth to a child. It would have been impossible for her husband to have been the father of her unborn child.

"After I learned that my niece had mysteriously left Baton Rouge for New York, I decided to try to find her—tracking her down, so to speak, in much the same manner you found me. Since the death of my brother, I have considered myself my niece's guardian. My niece's closest friend, a girl with whom she had gone to college, lived in Brooklyn Heights. It didn't take too much detective skill for me to figure out that was where I ought to start my search.

"I arrived in Brooklyn several days after the baby was born. My niece's friend begged me not to go to the hospital right away, fearing that it might be too much of a shock for the mother, who had carefully planned the birth to take place in secret so as to avoid causing dismay or shame to members of the family. I could understand her feelings. I have one or two relatives who, to paraphrase old Heywood Broun, were prudes to the point where they would put pants on horses if they could.

"All I wanted to do was to put my arms around the girl and tell her we'd be glad to have her move in with us and that we'd be happy to make any arrangement that would meet her needs. We were even prepared to adopt the baby if she wished us to. But by the time I was able to get to her—this was several days after we arrived—she had already carried out her plan. It had been previously arranged with an adoption agency that the baby would be turned over to its new parents as soon as conditions permitted following birth.

"When I saw my niece at the hospital, the first thing I did, of course, was to reassure her that we would stand by her whatever the circumstances. She was warm and affectionate in her responses but told us there was no way of altering the plans for the baby. She did, however, agree to return to Elkhart to live with us.

"We had no knowledge of the whereabouts of the baby. My niece had resolved to say nothing about the matter. She continued to live with us until 1965, when she died in a flash fire at the community school where she had been teaching. There seemed no end to the tragedies that, generation after generation, had stalked our family.

"Sometime in 1967, I read in the newspapers about the child chess prodigy, Paul Glover. It didn't seem possible that it was our boy, but the age was exactly the same. The orphanage was in Brooklyn. And most of all, there was the almost supernatural chess ability. It didn't detract any from my hunches or my excitement that the name should have been Paul. Eerie, wasn't it, that his foster parents should have named him Paul? Pure coincidence, of course. I knew I would have to see the boy and bring him back home.

"The moment I met the child I knew he belonged to our family. On our side, he had the characteristic shape of head. But his eyes—my God, those eyes. . . . If you ever saw any of the portraits of Paul Morphy, you would never forget those deep-set, brooding eyes. When you looked at them it was like looking into a dark eternity.

"In talking to the orphanage people, I learned that they had become increasingly concerned over Paul's difficulty in developing his language skills. Even the way he played with alphabet blocks worried them.

"I asked the orphanage director whether Paul had overcome his reading problems and learned that the child was severely dyslexic. I was distressed at this, but the account of the disability provided the final confirmation about the fact that he was my grand-nephew. Paul Morphy had suffered from dyslexia and had to be read to until he was almost seventeen. My brother—the child's grandfather—was also dyslexic.

"Young Paul still doesn't read. He has to go to a special school. I've used all the professional knowledge at my own command to help the boy. We've still got a long way to go. I can't say that he will ever read. But we've got to continue to try to help him as much as we can. I'm sure he's not retarded even though he still speaks in partially formed sentences and has a very limited vocabulary."

The professor's wife poured fresh coffee. Up to this point, I could hardly take in what I had been hearing; the account was such a mixture of the bizarre and the poignant as to seem unimaginable. When the professor reached for his coffee I thought this was a good time to ask the obvious question: How could a child whose intelligence was so limited be a genius at chess?

"Clinically speaking it is quite possible," the professor said. "Whatever his inability to read or articulate, he has a most extraordinary memory. They say this is the one attribute that great chess players have in common."

"What about the boy's interest in chess?" I asked. "Has he had any opportunity to play?"

The professor leaned forward in his chair. Again, the same intense, direct look. When he spoke, the note of awe in his voice was unmistakable.

"Something rather unbelievable happened back there in Brooklyn when Paul, at the age of eight, was playing and beating the best players in the Metropolitan area. In one of those games, Paul made a terrifying discovery about the game. He discovered a fatal flaw in the basic construction of chess."

"A fatal flaw?"

"Yes, a fatal flaw. For hundreds, perhaps thousands of years, the game of chess has remained constant. No one knows exactly how the game originated. It has been the subject of countless myths and legends. The wise men of ancient India thought the game had been conceived by Vishnu. It is strange, is it not, that few people who play chess have ever questioned its basic design, as though it had been fashioned by the gods. But no one—that is, no one until this child—had ever discovered a weakness or misconception in the way the game is played—a weakness that can take away all its beauty and even its reason for being. And the moment Poop uncovered this flaw, he lost interest.

"There is something else. I believe he gave up the game because of his contempt for the people who are addicted to it. Frankly, he thought chess players were rather stupid. He couldn't understand why something that was so obvious to him shouldn't have been perceived by everyone who pretended to know the game."

I could feel the short hairs standing up on the back of my neck. Chess—infallible and immutable since the earliest historical records, recognized almost universally as the perfect game—had lost its mysteries to a child who couldn't read, who could barely construct a sentence, but who was now in a position to discredit and perhaps demolish a historic pastime because he had discovered a flaw in the fundamental design. I thought of the profound pleasure the game had brought to numberless people throughout history. Yet here was a boy who could spoil it all. My emotion of awe began to sour; I could feel my indignation boiling up.

"Why is it important that this flaw be made known?" I asked. "This game has gone on for centuries in the form it has now. Why not let it continue? Why shouldn't the secret stay with Paul?"

"That's just the point," the professor said. "Let me tell you something. The same day I brought Paul here from the orphanage, I tried to make him feel at home. I set up a chessboard and invited him to play. He looked at me with a sadness I don't think I can ever put out of my mind. 'No more game,' he said. I asked him to show me what he meant. 'Game no more good,' he said. Then he tried to show me why. Playing his white, he began with the standard pawn-to-king-four openings. Then, within four moves and without the loss of a major piece, he was able to prevent my castling. It happened so fast that I didn't immediately catch its significance. Everyone knows, of course, that a player who is willing to sacrifice a bishop— it's called the Danish gambit—can sacrifice the piece and prevent his opponent from castling. But this price is generally regarded as too high; that's why the Danish gambit is considered unsound. I don't want to tell you—at least, not right now—exactly how young Paul did it without giving up a bishop. It's a little complicated but impossible to guard against."

"What if he has the black pieces?" I asked.

"Same thing. We played a second game. Paul had black. I was determined to use my advantage of moving first to bring about my castling as quickly as possible. No use. Paul was able to exploit his special knowledge of the tragic flaw in chess on both sides of the board. Since castling is an integral part of chess, its elimination from the game also spoils the game."

"You haven't answered my question," I said. "Why does the secret have to be exposed? Who, other than you, knows about Paul's discovery?"

"No one," the professor said. "At least, not so far as I am aware."

"Then why not just keep the secret to yourself?"

"Assume I do. But that doesn't meet the problem. I'm seventy-six years old. Paul is only twelve. I can probably prevent the secret from becoming known while I'm alive. Then what? At some point Paul's bound to tell what he knows. When he does, it will destroy the game."

"But you indicated that he gave up the game as soon as he discovered the great flaw. If he doesn't play again, perhaps there will be no occasion for him to disclose his secret."

"Yes—Paul has been playing again—but not simple chess as you and I know the game. In order to sustain his interest, he has constructed four sets of three-dimensional chess. Try to follow me in this. Each of these constructions is played in cubistic depth rather than on a flat surface. And, since he has four such sets, he contrives somehow to interrelate all the games. Mathematically, it requires a computer to calculate the number of decisions he has to make for each move. Figure it out for yourself if you can. There is the linear board. Then, the board is played as a cube. Then the cube is played against other cubes."

It was completely beyond me. I could understand, however, the main point. The boy had managed to find a level at which his capacity to play chess could be fully engaged. But how did he construct the game so that he could play against himself?

"I have watched him carefully," the professor said. "He has no interest in playing against living opponents. What he apparently does is to imagine that he's playing against several grand masters at one time. For example, he has studied the styles of players like Alekhine, Capablanca, Lasker, and Morphy—yes, especially Morphy. Then he projects himself into the style of each man—in order to play against them simultaneously."

"But I thought you said he couldn't read."

"Correct, but he does have facility with numbers. And, since the games of the grand masters have all been recorded with numerical notations, he has been able to familiarize himself with their styles. I've been buying him books with the records of tournament games."

The professor waved at a row of books on the lower shelf.

I had been told far more than I dreamed of learning about Paul Glover. But why had the professor confided so fully in me? I put the question to him.

"I told you just a moment ago I was seventy-six. My wife and I are the only ones who know the full story. Maybe it isn't important whether anyone else knows it. Has it occurred to you to wonder what will happen to young Paul after we are gone? Who will look after him? Also, it is important for someone to do what he can to keep Paul from destroying chess."

Surely the professor wasn't thinking of me. He was scrutinizing me closely and he detected my thinly disguised consternation.

"I know all about you, having checked you out after the call from the orphanage. You and your wife have only one son, now twelve," the professor said. "You are in your thirties. When you were in high school you won a national good citizenship award. You were an orphan yourself. In any event, I am hoping to find someone who would be willing to look after Paul when we are gone. The only inducement I can offer you is to make available to you the story of his life and leave it to you to determine the circumstances of publication. You will agree with me, I am sure, that Paul may be the possessor of one of the most unusual minds in the world today. In all my years as a child psychologist I have known no case to compare with this one. I have studied the literature and find no instance in which intelligence has run so rampant in one direction while being apparently retarded in all others. It is not unusual, of course, to find men who are masters at chess but are dullards in everything else. Some of them are quite boorish. Boorishness, of course, is not a concomitant of ignorance. But, for some reason, quite a few chess champions have been incomparably lacking in the graces that go with a civilized mind. Young Paul's propensity for being rude is, I fear, rather large and typical.

"What I am trying to say is that this child is going to get into the history books someday. He could do it as a world chess grand master. Of course, he would have to conceal his special knowledge of the tragic flaw in chess.

If he did this, he could probably make a career for himself as the greatest grand master in chess who ever lived. Right now, it is possible he could take on Fischer, Botvinnik, Spassky, or Tal. Apart from chess, he could, I suppose, offer himself for clinical study. There isn't a research center in the world involved in brain study that would not jump at the chance to put him under observation. As Paul's legal guardian, you should find it all very diverting and productive."

My mind was spinning. I had come to Elkhart in search of a story and I was being propositioned to accept custody of a human oddity. Then, out of the corner of my eye I saw young Paul standing just outside the study door. I caught a glimpse of his terror-stricken young face. I realized that the child had been aware of what was being said. He looked at me, too. In that second or two during which our eyes met, we communicated our mutual help-lessness and uncertainty. Then, very quickly, the boy turned and went out the front door, never to return.

Several months ago, the professor telephoned to ask my help in checking out two reports about a teenager playing park-bench chess that had just come in—one from New Orleans, the other from Minneapolis. We agreed that the professor would go to Minneapolis and I to New Orleans. I flew down to New Orleans and went directly to the Latin Quarter, where I visited the old Morphy home, now officially under the protective care of the landmarks commission. I was taken on a tour of the house. What caught my eye most of all was a portrait of Paul Morphy, dark-eyed and brooding. The resemblance around the eyes to young Paul Glover was almost supernatural.

I learned from the guide that a young boy of fourteen or so had come to visit the place only a week or so earlier.

He moved very slowly from room to room, the guard said, as though recapturing old memories.

From the Morphy house, I went to the public square not far away. Several men on park benches were playing chess. I described Paul and asked if they had seen him. One of them said that a boy fitting that description had played blindfolded against him and two other men only three days earlier and had won $1.50. It was a phenomenal performance, they said. They had asked the boy if he would be coming back the following day. The boy shook his head, not changing expression. He hadn't been seen since.

I asked if the boy had used a succession of moves at the start of each game to prevent castling by his opponent. They said not.

What this meant to me was that Paul had decided—at least thus far—not to divulge his secret. It meant, too, that he had no intention of wrecking the game that could enable him to make a living.

That trip to New Orleans was almost a year ago. Except for the sporadic reports I mentioned a moment ago, nothing has been heard about young Paul.

Of one thing I am certain: Before too many years there will be a new chess champion in the world or the game itself will cease to exist as we have known it, for he will have revealed the ease with which castling can be blocked without penalty, thus invalidating a feature of the game that is as fundamental as the characteristics of a rook or even a queen. For the sake of countless millions of chess players all over the world, now alive and yet to be born, I hope it is the former.

In any case, it is a profoundly unsettling thought to me that a teenager should be at large in the world, the future of chess in his hands—or, more precisely, in his compartmentalized brain.

Personals

WILL THE YOUNG MAN who sang the aria from La Forza del Destino on the Michigan Boulevard bus in Chicago on March 11, 4:30 PM please identify himself. I have a job opening in my "Spaghetti and Song" restaurant. SR/W Box PS.

CONFOUND YOUR FRIENDS with our shrinking tablecloths. They will start the meal with an exquisite full-size table covering (up to 8 by 6 feet). The tablecloth shrinks at an almost imperceptible rate until it is the size of a napkin. SR Box NK.

DON'T BE EMBARRASSED by your parrot's gastronomic imitations. Our researchers have devised a simple food that produces contractions in your parrot's tongue and inhibits rude burplike noises. Burp-Free Parrot Food, Inc. SR Box FB.

COMPUTER ERROR has resulted in 96,000 men's shirts with 40-inch sleeves and size 13 collars. All colors and patterns. Willing to sell or trade entire lot to highest bidder. SR Box MW.

6

A Sitewell Variorum

SUPERHIGHWAY OVER THE MISSISSIPPI

Sir:

Is no one going to raise a voice against the plan to erect a ten-lane elevated superhighway over the full length of the Mississippi River—from its upper reaches in Minnesota to the Gulf of Mexico? Or are we to believe that most people assume that a project conceived in such arrogant and monumental stupidity cannot possibly survive past the first round of debate?

We wrote to the U.S. Department of Transportation, pointing out the obvious: namely, that the Mississippi River does not drop down through the country in a straight line but describes beautiful loops and twists in the course of its heralded journey through the heart of America. Think of the billions of dollars, we wrote, that would be required to build a continuous highway over all these turnings and loopings. The Department of Transportation tried to reassure us by saying it had no intention of building over every twist in the Mississippi River. What it intended to do was to straighten out the river first. This is even worse than the original cockamamie highway idea. Straightening out the Mississippi!

Some people, if given half a chance, would probably try to straighten out the smile on the Mona Lisa.

Saturday Review has demonstrated leadership capacity in the conservation field with its *Environment Newsletter*. Is it too much to hope that *SR* will sound the alarm that may yet save the Mississippi?

We, the undersigned, have been on opposite sides during major public debates in the past, but we join together now in this appeal to the pride every American must feel in his magnificent heritage.

K. Jason Sitewell
A. F. Day
New York, N.Y.

WHERE HAVE ALL THE ARMORIES GONE?

Sir:

Is there any symbol of security as comforting as that of an old armory? I think of all the years I commuted to work from Connecticut each morning with a comfortable and protected feeling because the road to the railroad station took me past the old armory on the corner of the old Boston Post Road and Route 123. I would look up at the massive walls and cannon turrets of the old armory and all my fears about Communist or Fascist invaders would be put to rest.

Then one day, I noticed scaffolding going up on the armory. A sign, off in a corner and so small that hardly anyone noticed it, disclosed the fact that the armory was being torn down to make way for a spur that would connect the Connecticut Turnpike to Route 7. Nothing was said concerning a new location for the armory. Nothing, apparently, was to take its place. What about the security it provided?

I decided to move my family to Manhattan—in the shadow of the magnificent armory on Park Avenue and 34th street. The walls were even thicker and higher than at the Norwalk armory. The gun-and-cannon turrets were even more formidable. And a lookout tower rose a hundred feet or more from the top level of the armory—a magnificent red-brick shaft that reached into the sky and imparted a heavenly quality to the citizen's feelings of personal security. I never had the good fortune to ascend the tower, but I was certain that it commanded a view of all the approaches to the New York harbor and that the tower sentries could readily discern any attacking forces.

Apart from its value against invaders by sea, the Park Avenue armory had an immediate capability against land enemies. Even though part of the city might be invaded or seized, citizens could hole up inside and help beat back attempts to scale the walls.

But the 34th Street armory is scheduled to be torn down. Who made the decision? What does it portend? Why was not the citizenry informed? Secretary of Defense

Melvin Laird is probably a sincere anti-Communist, but his failure to speak up in defense of the armories is unsettling in the extreme. Where does the new Secretary of Defense, Elliot Richardson, stand in the matter? What about President Nixon himself? Ordinarily, his visit to Peking might be explained in terms of a new containment policy against the Soviet Union, but considered in the context of his silence on the armory question, the new China policy is disconcerting, to say the least.

Not even the Birch Society has exhibited any tremors about the decline of the armories. What has happened to the nation's defenders? What has happened to patriotism? And where will we play tennis during the winter months?

K. Jason Sitewell

FATAL DECISION

Sir:

The action of the state of Michigan in converting cemeteries into golf courses may appeal to that small but powerful segment of our population that invests the sport with spiritual significance, but it is dreadful public policy nevertheless. The fact that the people of Michigan were given an opportunity to vote on this proposition, and decided in favor of it, doesn't make it right. I find it difficult to conceive of any circumstances that could justify seeding over a cemetery. Nor am I reassured by the fact that the Michigan graves, by being relocated and stacked, will be preserved in 1/100 the space. Even if the purpose had nothing to do with golf and sought to build schools or hospitals, I would still be against it.

There is something fiendishly symbolic in this entire

enterprise. Any civilization that has so little respect for the dead can hardly be expected to have respect for the living. If the Michigan abomination is allowed to stand, then no grave anywhere is safe.

K.J.S.
Grand Rapids, Mich.

REVOLUTIONARY ANCESTORS

Sir:

The *Saturday Review* is to be congratulated on its two Bicentennial issues. No other magazine that I know of has featured what is actually the most important aspect of your American Revolution: namely, the way it changed the world, and not just America.

Ever since coming to the United States as Special Professor of Russian Studies, I have been doing work on the ancestry of the American Founding Fathers. Their genealogy is generally concentrated in England, as has been documented in numerous biographies. Less well known, however, is the fact that both Washington and Jefferson are of collateral Russian ancestry. Washington's great-grandmother was pure Russian (Yulia Mayarova). Jefferson's grandfather on his mother's side was half-Russian (Taras Fyodorov). Thomas Paine had at least two Russian ancestors no more than three generations removed (Alexei Turishieff and Georgii Manshikov).

I also have some preliminary evidence that the Adams family had distant collateral origins in Russia.

Obviously, these genealogical lines are too thin for Russians to claim credit for the founding of the United States. But it is a source of pride to Russians in your

Bicentennial year that they were at least part of your noble heritage.

Prof. Alexandre K. J. Sitwelof
Cambridge, Mass.

THE ABOLITION OF CHRISTMAS CARDS

Sir:

Readers of this magazine may recall my earlier communications about Congressman A. F. Day of California, whose proposed items of legislation, if enacted, would have produced incalculable injury or injustice to large segments of the American populace, especially those whose basic welfare is tied to regular visitations to golf courses.

Congressman Day now has thirty-seven members of the House of Representatives as cosponsors of a bill that would have the effect of abolishing Christmas cards and substituting a computerized registry that, he contends, would annually save the American people many millions of dollars.

The core of the argument is not without merit. Congressman Day believes that Christmas cards have become a soulless form of social tyranny, resented by the sender and often ignored by the receiver. He has calculated that, in an average year, 87,000 tons of paper are consumed in the manufacture of Christmas cards. He is disturbed by the fact that, at a time when our forests are being rapidly depleted, the American people cut down 2,141,000 trees last year in order to accommodate a convention that most people, if asked anonymously, would prefer not to sustain. Moreover, the postage bill alone for Christmas cards in 1976 came to $130 million.

Almost half the Christmas cards sent in 1976 carried no signatures or handwritten messages of any kind. The names of the senders were printed on the cards. The procedure was as personal (and meaningful) as popcorn coming out of a vending machine.

Congressman Day recognizes, of course, that the custom has gone on for such a long time that any single individual is hesitant to defy it, lest friends attach mistaken significance to the absence of his or her cards in the Christmas mail. Both sender and recipient, therefore, are locked into a grim game that no one particularly appreciates, but that all must play because the onus applies to the person who takes the first step in withdrawing from it.

Congressman Day has come up with a scheme that he believes is ecologically valuable and socially workable. His bill (H.R. 9713A) would establish a national computerized Christmas greeting registry.

The steps in the process are very simple.

First, Christmas cards would be abolished by law.

Second, a national computerized Christmas greeting registry would be created by an Act of Congress.

Third, each individual who wished to save the expense of mailing Christmas cards would simply send a list of names of the intended recipients to the computerized Christmas card registry. A nominal charge of $3.50 would cover the cost of registering up to one hundred names. Additional names could be registered at the same rate $3.50 per hundred. These names would then be computerized into a master printout.

Fourth, those who wished to know what cards they would have received, and from whom, would have only to write to the Christmas greeting computer registry, enclosing $5.00. They would receive computerized printouts of the names of all persons who wished them well at Christmas and the New Year and had paid to have this information recorded.

Fifth, the printout sheet would have your own name and address in the upper-left-hand corner, immediately below which, in prominent and underlined type, would be this heading:

Here is a list of names of all those persons greeting you at Christmas as well as wishing you well for the New Year.

Sixth, if you wished to reciprocate by returning the Christmas and New Year's greetings the following year, it would not be necessary to save last year's printout. You would need only to instruct the registry to send your greetings to all those who "sent" you greetings the previous year.

Seventh, a significant feature of the plan is that any individual could have his or her name removed confidentially from the list of any sender for only fifty cents. The government would not divulge the names of any persons requesting such removal, but would inform the sender that he is entitled to replace a specified number of names because of anonymous withdrawals.

I recognize, as does A. F. Day, the artificiality and overcommercialization of Christmas, of which the greeting card with the printed name of the sender is such a deplorable manifestation. But the notion of computerized printouts as a substitute is unhappily symbolic of the increasing dehumanization of our society. Bad as it is to chop down a tree, it is infinitely worse to assign to a computer those benevolent and warm impulses of spirit for which Christmastime provides such a needed and rare outlet.

I trust your editorial page will oppose H.R. 9713A and that your readers will not hesitate to urge their congressmen to vote against the bill.

K. Jason Sitewell
New York, N.Y.

ॐ

Sir:

Would you vote yes on Bill 9713A,
Abolishing by law all Christmas cards?
That's what's proposed. A congressman named Day,
Would substitute computerized regards,
Sent nationally, by Greeting Registry,
Oh, yes, we'd save . . . on postage stamps alone,
On tons of paper . . . ergs of energy . . .
Computers though! They'd turn all cards to stone—
Squeeze dry whatever message sent.
We don't need to be dehumanized;
We need the loving spirit of Advent,
Exactly what the Christmas tide provides.
So here's to those traditions we revere
And a joy filled, rewarding year.

Margaret Shardelow Young

DOUBLE JEOPARDY

Sir:

Some years ago, talk of Quebec's splitting off from Canada was dismissed as a species of political nonsense. Yet we now find that a separate Quebec is a serious political prospect, carrying the danger of a chain reaction of secessionist movements in other Canadian provinces as well.

It is not too early, therefore, for the American people to oppose resolutely the secessionist efforts now starting up on the tiny island of LaFlore, southeast of Savannah.

The people of LaFlore—like their brethren from Martha's Vineyard, who were making similar noises last summer—have announced their intention to join up with France, thus giving the Québecois an important ally on the Atlantic Coast. Although no more than 12 kilometers square, LaFlore does have a certain potential for causing trouble with the American mainland. Unknown to many, the island is, at its centermost part, the world's largest single source of nutrium. Nutrium, as we know, is the principal ingredient in the production of satellite nuclear trigger systems, the failure of which, and consequences therefrom, have become all too familiar to our northern neighbor in the past few months.

Obviously, the encouragement being offered by the French government to Quebec as well as to LaFlore separatists has ominous implications for the United States. The fact that Congressman A. F. Day has openly supported independence for LaFlore is reason enough to be alarmed.

How, one might ask, can the 5,000 residents of a nonstrategic stretch of offshore beach defend their bid for autonomy against overwhelming American power? The answer is surprisingly simple, as witness this recent statement by Representative Day's good friend, the governor of LaFlore, Henri de la Imholtz: "Let's face it. If you've got nutrium, you've got the bomb."

Nothing could be more hazardous than for Americans to ignore the tendencies now observable in LaFlore. Today's absurdities have a way of becoming tomorrow's realities.

K. Jason Sitewell
New York, N.Y.

Book Review

The Darwinian Inversion
BY STEFAN BRONOWICZ
AYEFF DAYE PRESS, DUBLIN,
466 PP., $8.00

Professor Bronowicz presents additional evidence to support the thesis to which he has devoted his entire professional life: namely, that apes are an offshoot, and not the progenitors, of the human race. This book contains photographs of artifacts and skeletons which, according to carbon-14 tests, are more than 250,000 years old and which, Professor Bronowicz contends, verify the hypothesis of a Darwinian inversion. Essentially, this hypothesis holds that the Earth a long time ago was subjected to a series of violent shocks, accompanied by a high level of radioactivity, and that the effect on human genes was to produce a vast quantity of monsters, or what we commonly regard as apes, monkeys, and baboons. The only material presented by Dr. Bronowicz that is different from that contained in his previous works has to do with DNA skeins observed under electron microscopes. These human skeins or strands, when subjected to bombardment by radioactive uranium isotopes, bear a close relationship to existing skeins taken from living apes and monkeys. Despite the respectful attention being given to his work by the "New Anthropologists" of the British Institute of Biological Studies, Dr. Bronowicz's theories are not likely to upset the prevailing views.

K. Jason Sitewell

APING HUMANS

Sir:

Please cancel my subscription to *SR/W*. I was shocked beyond imagining when I read the review of *The Darwinian Inversion* by Stefan Bronowicz [Books in Brief, April 6]. I don't care how much evidence Mr. Bronowicz presents. The notion that the human species is not descended from apes but gave rise to apes is so far afield that I almost become apoplectic when I even think of it. No matter what the so-called New Anthropologists of the British Institute may say, I submit that this new theory is completely without scientific foundation and that it should never have been published, let alone reviewed by *SR/W*.

George Hammers
Chicago, Ill.

ॐ

Sir:

So glad to see K. Jason Sitewell back among the ranks of *SR/World* contributors—we've missed him.

Spotting his name in the April 6 issue's table of contents, I turned at once to his review on page 31 of *The Darwinian Inversion*—a work that would seem to expound a theory that I have long secretly held: "namely, that apes are an offshoot . . . of the human race." In support of this theory, may I suggest that Mr. Sitewell might well be cited as one of the most notorious monkeys on record?

And a Happy Ayeff Daye to you, too!

Gabrielle Griswold
Waban, Mass.

Book Review

Illegal Separation
BY A. A. SCANLON
AYEFF DAYE PRESS, DUBLIN,
676 PP. $6

The noted British scholar who has specialized in the relations between Great Britain and the American colonies presents a striking thesis in this book. He has analyzed all the documents involved in the separation between Great Britain and the thirteen American states and has identified no fewer than 816 illegalities and irregularities. His conclusion is that the separation has no legal standing and that the United States Constitution is itself unconstitutional. In fact, he believes that a case brought by the British government before the U.S. Supreme Court might produce a fascinating historical contretemps.

Specifically, what evidence does Professor Scanlon offer? He points out that Philip Maybeck, who signed all the auxiliary papers of separation for the colonies, was not authorized to act by either Rhode Island or Maine, yet proceeded to do so. In fact, Maybeck's participation in the proceedings was repudiated by both states, thus invalidating the document altogether, but no substitute document carrying an authorized signature was executed or even prepared. Still another irregularity was that the New York State Legislature, for some unknown reason, routinely referred the ratification papers to committee along with fifteen supporting documents. When the group of materials was returned from committee, the central document, inexplicably, was unsigned. Professor Scanlon believes that the omission was an act of sheer carelessness, but the fact remains that the separation documents were legally incomplete. He considers the argument that only New York, Rhode Island, and Maine, because of these irregularities, should be regarded as still part of the Crown, leaving the rest of the United States legally intact; but he makes two points in this connection. First, the agreement among the colonies called for them to act as a single entity. Second, the supporting documents ratified by the New York State Legislature were contingent upon their collective legality, which the Rhode Island and Maine repudiatory actions completely negated.

Is there any suggestion of deliberate intent by Philip Maybeck to sabotage the separation procedures? Professor Scanlon publishes a facsimile of a letter by Maybeck's widow to a friend in Liverpool. The letter says that immediately after signing the articles of separation, Maybeck informed his wife that he was going abroad on a confidential mission for about a year. When he returned, he disclosed to his wife that he had successfully invested in some business ventures in Liverpool. Professor Scanlon went to the trouble of inspecting the Liverpool town clerk's record of business listings during the period and has found nothing to support the argument that Maybeck's sudden wealth was the result of any known business undertaking. Had Maybeck, in the parlance of contemporary political affairs, been paid off? If so, why has the British government never questioned the legality of the separation? More pointed still, why did Great Britain not lay claim to Rhode Island, Maine, and New York, at the very least? Did British government officials have a sudden change of heart about the entire affair? Were they just as happy to let the entire matter drop?

One way or the other, if the treaties of separation between the two countries lack validity because they were illegally executed, does this mean that the "United States"—the use of the quotation marks is deliberate—is actually still part of the British Empire and that Americans, who regard themselves as U.S. citizens, have been living out a historical fiction? Does it mean that Americans are still subject to British taxation? If so, how far back does this liability extend? Five years? Fifty years? One hundred and ninety years? Is there no statute of limitations that can be applied? Under which body of law— British or American? The complications are endless. Can the British, armed with a U.S. Supreme Court order, proceed to dip into what Americans have always regarded as their national treasury? And what about Fort Knox? Could a British court order empty our gold reserves? Does ownership of all our military stockpiles pass to the British?

How seriously can we take Professor Scanlon's thesis? Even if we accept the accuracy of his research, it would be profoundly awkward at this late date even to catalog all the complications involved in undoing almost two hundred years of separate but illegal nationhood. Our guess is that neither the Americans nor the British will have the stomach or, quite frankly, the intellectual candlepower to unscramble so much history. Inevitably, one wishes that

Professor Scanlon would withdraw his book. It is difficult to see what useful purpose can be served by having these questions raised at this time.

K. Jason Sitewell

ᙖ

Sir:

Reacting once again with panic in place of reason, in his review of Professor Scanlon's *Illegal Separation* [*SR*, 4/5/75], K. Jason Sitewell displays a monumental ignorance of the most glorious period of our nation's history. In fact, as the eminent constitutional scholar A. F. Day points out in his recent *A Time of Fools* (U. M. I. M. Press, 1975), not only did the Thirteen Colonies separate from England in a perfectly lawful manner, but at the same time contracted to accept her as number fourteen.

What now, Sitewell?

Ronald Jacobowitz
Phoenix, Ariz.

ᙖ

Sir:

It is good to have K. Jason Sitewell back on the pages of the *Saturday Review*. I dare say that no one but Sitewell would have been likely to run across so provocative—and encouraging—a book as *Illegal Separation* by A. A. Scanlon. Certainly no one else could have reviewed the book in as informative a fashion as did Sitewell in your April 5 issue. Having said this, I must disagree with his conclusion that we should let sleeping dogs lie.

The prospect that the American Revolution was illegal and that we may be still a colony of Great Britain provides a good deal of hope at a rather dreary period of our history. We should jump at the chance to regain our lost colonyhood and be wary of the nationalist hotheads who will soon be urging that we seek some sort of commonwealth status similar to that of Canada. Let us avoid this trap and insist that we hold our full rights as a colonial possession of Great Britain.

Let me point out a few modest ways in which this status would improve things for us here in the United States immediately. As a young nation not quite two hundred years old we are embarrassed and uncomfortable at slipping into a postindustrial society. As a colony of Great Britain we could overnight be proud that we are still able to waste our natural resources so prodigally.

We are about to get into a nasty fight over a national health program. That would be behind us, not ahead of us, when we rejoin the Empire.

We are, or some of us at least, plagued with guilt over killing women and children in Japan with the A-bomb, of losing China to the Chinese, and recently over the unhappy outcome of our adventures in Southeast Asia. With the charge of the Light Brigade at Balaklava and Neville Chamberlain's "peace in our time" agreement with Hitler in our history we could easily shrug off misjudgments like Vietnam.

There is not space in this communication to catalog all of the benefits of colonial status. Uppity women could join a major political party headed by one of our own.

For nearly two hundred years we have been trying to make taxation with representation work and I think all of us would be happier to return to taxation *without* representation. Then someone else, not us, would be responsible for the inequities which bear down on us every April 15.

All the world would be playing the same size golf ball. Sports fans who find the fast pace of baseball unnerving would be able to turn on TV and watch the soothing sport of cricket.

And, speaking of TV, since the BBC would be our very own, we could turn off its programs instead of being forced to watch them on underpowered public broadcasting stations because they are Culture imported from an older country. I suppose the change would make Alistair Cooke a man without a country, but then you can't have everything.

There are also economic benefits. Our problem in the States (if we are still the States) is that we keep figuring out how to make more and more things with fewer people. This causes unemployment, which right now is a very serious problem. But the British are masters at using a lot of people and taking a long time to make fewer things. Consider as one example the amount of British labor that goes into making a man's suit. Wearing suits of twenty-ounce material that are too tight in the armpits would be a small price to pay for the increased employment that would result. Or, suppose we continue to buy the same number of automobiles, but have them made by British manufacturing techniques. This will require enough manpower to bring all of the laid-off auto workers back to the factory and more besides (some may say that America has too many cars in running condition now, but that condition won't last for long when we take up driving on the left side of the road).

A few adjustments may take a little time. When the New York subways become as efficient as the underground, its patrons might be uneasy for a while, riding in trains that run on time and are not embellished with graffiti. Some may be uncomfortable in double-decker buses and have a hard time adjusting to paying fare only for the distance they ride, but some of us, old enough to remember double-decker buses in American cities, will like the change.

I suppose there will be a few minor problems. For one thing, I can't for the life of me figure out what we should do about the DAR.

Nonetheless, I think we all owe thanks to K. Jason Sitewell for offering us a vision of hope at a time when, as one of our leaders told us just the other day, we stand at a crossroads of history.

Our Mother Country has never stood at this crossroads because it has always been too occupied with muddling through to pause at such a dangerous place. I hope I will not sound disloyal when I suggest that none of our recent presidents could hold a candle to Wilson or Heath when it comes to muddling.

God save our Gracious Queen and God bless K. Jason Sitewell.

Samuel C. Brightman
Washington, D.C.

P.S.: I would suggest that Sitewell might consider confining his writing to public affairs. Recently he wrote in a golfing publication about an Australian aborigine of about my age who made two consecutive holes-in-one driving across the ocean on a hole similar to the 16th at Cyprus Point, where I have emptied my bag of cut balls hitting a driver for the green after taking the coward's path with my competition ball. Since I have been having some difficulty with my tee shots, I dug out of the attic an old walking stick which my grandfather had cut from a dwarf graphite tree in Pennsylvania during the War Between the States. The walking stick seemed to fit the description of the club used by the aborigine in Sitewell's article and I carefully imitated the striking action as he described it. The ball I stroked was the new Whap DX 6 with the frozen kaopectate center and torsion dimples. The ball soared 250 yards on the fly (somewhat longer than my normal drive), struck a rock in a creek just short of the out-of-bounds markers on the right-hand side of our first hole, bounced over two houses, struck the roadway, and ricocheted to the corner of Goldsboro Road and Bradley Boulevard, where it caused a three-vehicle accident involving an ambulance, a police cruiser, and a fire engine. Since then I have had some unpleasant correspondence with my insurance company, it is difficult for me to make up a foursome on Sundays, and my handicap has been disallowed for club tournaments. I think it accurate to say that Sitewell's brief article about golf has made more of a change in my game than the whole damn book by Ben Hogan about pronating the wrists. I am sure that Sitewell means to be helpful when he brings his unique knowledge of history and his ability for vivid description to the subject of golf, but I must confess that I have to consider that the results of reading his article in *Golf Digest* have been, for me at least, what Sitewell, with his ability always to find the *mot juste,* would call a mixed blessing.

Private Correspondence

July 14, 1975

S. C. Johnson & Son, Inc.
Racine, Wisconsin

Sirs:

I have seen your television commercial showing the difference in the sound level when you scrape an American Express card on two sides of a man's face after he uses Edge and a competitor's shaving cream.

It was, I must admit, a powerfully persuasive experience to see and hear the difference. After looking at the program I switched my membership to the Diner's Club and am glad to report that the scraping sound level on both sides of my face is exactly the same. How can I thank you?

K. Jason Sitewell

❧

July 22, 1975

Mr. K. Jason Sitewell
Saturday Review
488 Madison Avenue
New York, N.Y. 10022

Dear Mr. Sitewell:

Thank you for taking the time to write us. Compliments are always nice.

Our company has a long history of providing quality products—and we naturally plan to extend this same high quality to all of our products in the personal care field.

136

Letters like yours make us feel that we're on the right track.

Since, as the saying goes, one good turn deserves another—we're sending you a complimentary package of a couple of products. I hope you'll enjoy using them. I've also enclosed copies of a few booklets and pamphlets which might be of interest to you.

Joan Radke
Product Information
Specialist
Consumer Services Center
S. C. Johnson & Son, Inc.

᠊᠍

July 29, 1975

Dear Joan Radke:

I am grateful to you for your generous letter of July 22, replying to my letter thanking you for your television commercial in which you use an American Express card to demonstrate the superiority of Edge. You will recall that, thanks to your TV commercial, I changed to the Diner's Club, with the result that there is no longer any disparity between the scraping sound on the left side of my face and the right side of my face. I also notified the Diner's Club, which, understandably, would like everyone to know that the scraping sound discrepancy would disappear with the use of a DC card. It would be a very nice gesture, indeed, if you could inform people through your TV commercial that, if they are troubled about their special scraping sounds, simply switch to the Diner's Club.

I trust this will be helpful.

K. Jason Sitewell

꧁

July 30, 1975

Dear Ms. Radke:

This is a postscript to my letter of July 29. Since writing you yesterday, I made what I am sure you agree is a fascinating discovery. Instead of using either an American Express or Diner's Club card, I used a Jack of diamonds from a set of bridge playing cards. You will be pleased to know that it works just as well as American Express or Diner's. This means a savings of about $22, taking into account the average cost of a credit card.

Again, I want to thank you for making it all possible.

K. Jason Sitewell

P.S.: You probably have wondered whether any significance should be attached to the Jack of diamonds, and whether it would work just as well with any other card. Frankly, I am mystified myself about this. The other playing cards are all better than the credit cards, but, for some reason, the Jack of diamonds works best.

꧁

July 31, 1975

Dear Ms. Radke:

This is another note about your television commercial in which you use an American Express card to herald the virtues of Edge Shaving Cream. You suggested that people try the same test. I have done so, the result being that I now have a serious facial infection that makes it impossible for me to go to work. Meanwhile, I have these terrible doctor's bills and my wife no doubt finds it repugnant even to look at me.

Did you have any idea of the trouble you would cause when you told people to scratch their faces with Amex cards?

K. Jason Sitewell

ॐ

August 22, 1975

Dear Mr. Sitewell:

How very clever of you!

You have regaled us with your wit, you have entertained us with your knowledge of credit cards, and you have enthralled us with your stamina to try all fifty-two cards (or was it a double pinochle deck?) to determine that for you the Jack o' diamonds worked best.

We are distressed at your last letter because of the trouble, but you must not be using Edge because then there would be no scratching, right? Or maybe in a wild moment to try the test you inadvertently used a Queen of (Bleeding?) Hearts?

Best you check the deck next time if you persist in making the test after every shave, but do use Edge and join the thousands of satisifed users for the smooth shave, many of whom, alas, are without any credit or other cards to make any test, but who are confident enough in Johnson Wax products to be believers.

Joan Radke
Consumer Services Center

ॐ

139

September 2, 1975

Dear Miss Radke:

Your letter addressed to the late K. Jason Sitewell has come to my attention. It is my sad duty to inform you that Mr. Sitewell is deceased, the result of a facial infection. His bereaved mother tells me that the malady was caused originally by a television commercial in which you told people what to do with their Amex cards. I have lost a capable and devoted assistant.

Under the circumstances, I must look upon this entire incident with melancholy disfavor. I recognize you had no way of knowing, when you embarked upon this television series, that you would be cutting down in the prime of life an earnest young man whose only fault was that he took your advice.

Incidentally, our senior editor has looked into the matter and informs me that the polyethylene substance used in the manufacture of credit cards is highly toxic. Before another unspeakable tragedy occurs, perhaps you might find some way of counteracting the toxic properties in the cards. Either that, or devise another TV commercial that is just as convincing but somewhat less lethal.

Norman Cousins

Saturday Review
Attention: Mr. Norman Cousins

May these few words serve as an expression of deepest sympathy.

Joan Radke
Consumer Services Center

September 15, 1975

Dear Miss Radke:

Everyone in this office was deeply touched by your tender condolence message. K. Jason Sitewell was a valued colleague and we shall not soon see his like again. We are puzzled, however, that so intelligent a man could allow himself to be gulled by an insidious television commercial. He died, as you know, of a massive infection that began when he started scraping his face with a credit card. He undertook this bizarre action, we understand, at your suggestion. His widow and colleagues, as I say, are properly grateful to you for your sympathy, but they are troubled lest other worthy men (and also women in this age of galloping liberation) may be struck down in their prime as the result of your prompting on TV. Surely the time has come, in the name of mercy if not in the name of Sitewell, to withdraw your dangerous urging. How many more men must die of credit-card poisoning before you devise a new and infection-free sales message?

Norman Cousins

P.S.: All the men in this office, as a gesture of respect for Jason Sitewell, have renounced shaving altogether. The result is that the aesthetics of the office are all shot to hell.

P.P.S.: As a final and cruel irony to the whole affair, consider the fact that the mortician who prepared poor K.J.S.'s body used Johnson's Wax for the dead man's mustache.

Dear Miss Radke:

I am the personal physician of the late K. Jason Sitewell who died on August 30, 1975, of a massive infection caused by the scraping of a credit card against one side of his face. The physiological process involved here is readily explicable. Shaving by its very nature is an unnatural operation, producing thousands of invisible incisions. Each of the hair follicles on the face, when freshly cut by a razor, is in effect a minor wound in the sense that it is an open pathway, albeit temporary, to the general circulatory system. The plastic chemical substances involved in the manufacture of credit cards are antagonistic to human chemistry, as was recently confirmed in a U.S. Government report. In particular, there is an alteration in homeostasis in direct ratio to the size of the hair follicle apertures and the quantity of foreign matter admitted to the circulatory system. The particularized effects of such an intervention are marked by an increase in the count of white blood cells and a related increase in corticoid activity, both of which are reflected in elevated sedimentation time. The manifestation of these negative homeostatic influences are epithelial inflammation, impairment of platelet formation, alteration in normal clotting time, and bone marrow depression.

In this particular case, the usual therapeutic means were employed without producing the desired effect. The full range of antibiotic medicines was employed with progressive intensities but it was increasingly apparent that the malevolent effect of the plastic poison released into the bloodstream was unaffected by antipathological agents.

Unchecked, therefore, by the compounds available in the pharmaceutical armamentarium of the physician, the disease intensified rapidly. The sodium-potassium exchange was disrupted with a consequent drop in electrolytic activity, which in turn produced cardiac malfunctioning. Death came on the ninth day after the onset of the illness. The usual emergency measures to maintain oxygenization of the brain and continuous heart action were unavailing.

William M. Hitzig, M.D.

ह•

August 24, 1976

Mr. S. C. Johnson
Chairman and Chief Executive Officer
S. C. Johnson & Son, Inc.

Dear Mr. Johnson:

I am eager to receive confirmation from you of findings showing that the strange Legionnaires' disease in Philadelphia was caused by the scraping of polyethylene credit cards against freshly shaved faces, as you advise TV viewers to do in your Edge shaving-cream commercials.

I naturally thought of this possibility in connection with the Legionnaires' disease because of the remarkable similarity of symptoms with the symptoms of the late K. Jason Sitewell's illness. Mr. Sitewell was one of our employees whose terribly poignant death you may recall from our previous correspondence with Joan Radke of your Consumer Services Center. Mr. Sitewell, acting on the advice of your television commercial, scraped a credit card on both sides of his freshly shaven face. The pores were still open and the polyethylene entered the bloodstream, producing an agonizing death within a matter of days. I can understand the popularity of Edge with Legionnaires but I had not realized that so many of them would act on the basis of your television commercial. In any event, I am eager to learn from you whether you have undertaken an investigation to confirm the fact that the Legionnaires' disease was caused by the credit card test.

Harrison Smith

[Mr. Smith was, at that time, associate editor at the *Saturday Review.*]

ह~

September 17, 1975

Dear Ms. Radke:

I have been retained by the widow and family of K. Jason Sitewell, who died as the result of factors described in the enclosed medical report by W. M. Hitzig, M.D. Death was the result of massive inflammation caused by an action induced by your company's public statements. In particular, the deceased, acting on instructions given by your representatives on television, did cause the edge of a credit card to be scraped against the right side of his face immediately after shaving. The result was an infection which was uncontrollable by any known therapeutic agent or other modalities of medical intervention, as attested by the attached medical statement.

Accordingly, I have been asked to institute appropriate legal remedial action.

144

It is of course difficult to fix a price on human life—especially on a life as promising as the one that went by the name of K. Jason Sitewell. I leave it to you to suggest what a suitable resolution should be.

Carl Schaeffer
Schaeffer, Dale & Vogel
Attorneys and Counsellors
at Law
New York, N.Y.

২৵

September 24, 1975

Dear Miss Radke:

I am the president of the newly founded PAPACI (Protect the American People Against Credit-card Infections). In view of what we understand is the Johnson company's involvement in the Sitewell tragedy, we feel you will want to play an important part in the fulfillment of our program. In particular, we seek your cooperation in directing your advertising agency to include a cautionary statement to the effect that TV viewers are not to take your commercial literally, and that credit cards should be scraped against the face only on advice of physicians and with the appropriate therapeutic safeguards, such as the use of a peroxide salve base. We are eager to enlist your support in this direction.

Mrs. K. Jason Sitewell

২৵

Dear Ms. Radke:

In the spirit of Christmas, I am pleased to convey to you, on behalf of the widow and family of K. Jason Sitewell, as well as of the staff of *Saturday Review*, complete forgiveness in the matter of the terrible demise of our beloved associate.

The family has asked me to inform you that they absolve you fully for your part in causing Mr. Sitewell's untimely death.

I suggest that we consider this whole tragic episode as closed.

Norman Cousins

Personals

NATHAN DETROIT, JR. Charter parties discreetly arranged. Cabin cruisers, cargo planes, air-conditioned moving vans. A family tradition since 1902 and still rolling. SR Box VV.

STENOTYPE TRANSCRIPTS of the 1946 Omaha City Council meetings now available at the lowest prices anywhere. We will not be undersold. Fourteen volumes. Orders filled in the order received. SR Box DS.

DEAR JANET: Don't think of marriage as a matter of losing your independence. Think of it as gaining subordination. Please come back and give our honeymoon a fair chance. Walter.

COMPUTER ERROR MERCHANDISE. Odd pages of manual, *Fly Your Own Helicopter*, and even pages of

Be Your Own Voice Teacher, mistakenly printed, interspersed, and bound as one book. 11,000 copies offered at half-price. SR Box OB.

WE ARE RECALLING all our 1973 Venetian blinds for slight adjustment and apologize to all customers who have sustained finger injuries. Hometown Venetian Blinds. SR Box VH.

NOW AVAILABLE: Nondisposable expanding napkins, to match our shrinking tablecloths. SR Box NK.

WILL ATTRACTIVE redhaired girl who rushed out after spilling yellow mustard on my new suit at Burger Heaven, Madison & 51st Street, New York City, last St. Patrick's Day, kindly write SR Box DT.

EASTERN U.S. inhabitants: shorten your winter, prepare now for Groundhog Day, Feb. 2, 1976. Our brochure, *How to Raise Shadowless Groundhogs,* identifies caves and holes in Pennsylvania where you can find best of breed. Write SR Box SE.

TIRED OF FALSE flattery and false friends? For a refreshing experience in candor, let Honest John Forthright tell you in full detail what a shlemozel you are. SR Box HJF.

ATTENTION: A new society is being formed for descendants of Austin Mittredge, notorious English swindler and stagecoach thief, who came to America in 1652 and was one of the founders of Harvard University. SR Box CE.

CONFOUND YOUR SECRETARY with our undecipherable messages on memo pads marked "URGENT." SR Box SV.

UNFORTUNATE PROGRAMMING of computer has produced a large number of tennis racquets attached to curved pearl revolver handles. Will dispose of at least 150 specimens to highest bidder. SR Box CC.

HAVE YOU EVER WONDERED what you would do if Prime Minister Leonid Brezhnev paid a surprise visit to your home? We can teach you Russian in 1,350 easy lessons. If that fails, we can teach you to speak English with a heavy Russian accent. Box WM.

TO JOHN DUNN né Higgins-Goldfarb: Your public notice had a familiar ring of arrogance. Could you be my long-lost brother Bernie from Morristown? If so, mother has finally died and left us a bundle. 70/30, take it or leave it. Sincerely, B.P. Higgins-Goldfarb

FORTUNATE COMPUTER ERROR has made it necessary to recall all Baremore Swimsuit Co. ladies'

swimsuits, sizes 6 thru 12, because of chemical substance in synthetic fibers that cause suit to dissolve on contact with seawater. Unchlorinated pool water no problem. Full refund promptly provided. Baremore Swimsuit Co. SR Box BS.

PUBLIC NOTICE: Neither of the two classified notices from the two men who claim to be B. P. Higgins-Goldfarb is the real B.P.H.-G. I am the real B. P. Higgins-Goldfarb. In order to cut short the present chain reaction of confusion, I am changing my name to Joe Dunn, and will not be responsible for any debts of any sort contracted by the two gentlemen. This goes for their wives, too. Joe Dunn. SR Box JD.

WILL TRADE VALUABLE collection of varnished hooplets for facsimile set of Lady Chatterley's love letters. SR Box CL.

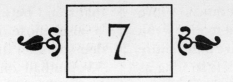

Charlie and Wilma

Of all K. Jason Sitewell's concoctions, none was sustained over a longer period of time than the saga of Charlie and Wilma, which began with a seemingly perfunctory notice in the Personals column of *SR* and ended in a party in living color in the editor's New York apartment, attended by several dozen readers of the magazine. What ultimately happened to Charlie and Wilma, as *Time* magazine might say, knows God.

WILMA. OF COURSE I love you and want to marry you and don't care if the entire world knows it so long as you know it, too. Please tell me where you are. I will live next to my mailbox until you do. Prayerfully, Charlie.

CHARLIE. I love you, too, but it's no use. Even if we didn't argue about Women's Lib and Watergate, they would be unspoken and would come between us. You've got to forget the month in Cannes and the trip to San Remo. You'll be all right. Wilma.

WILMA. For heaven's sake, if the only things that you think stand between us are Watergate and Women's Lib, I'll gladly embrace them both. Now, where in Sam Hill are you? Love, Charlie.

CHARLIE. It isn't only Watergate and Women's Lib that stand between us—it is also those dad-blame dog spots on the rug and TV football on Sundays. Love, Wilma.

CHARLIE. THIS IS MY LAST COMMUNICATION, and you needn't advertise again. I've met someone who will help me forget you. He's a mature New Zealander and he's taking me home with him next week. It's all for the best for both of us. Please believe me. Goodbye. Wilma.

WILMA. No, no, no; don't do it! But if you do, just know I'll be waiting for you always and thinking of what you said in San Remo. Entreatingly and everlastingly ever yours. Charlie.

WILMA. In cleaning the attic, I just discovered some letters to you from a guy named Harry. What goes? Charlie.

CHARLIE. Silly boy. "Harry" was just my old uncle, now deceased. I'm still going through with my plans for New Zealand. Wilma.

WILMA. I know for a fact that the man who lured you to New Zealand has separate families in West Hoboken and Nairobi. Please come back before this thing gets into the newspapers. Charlie.

WILMA. I don't want you to go off with that New Zealander but if you insist on going through with it, the least you can do is to return my baby pictures and cardigan sweater. Charlie.

CHARLIE. Who asked you to clean the attic? My relationship with Harry is none of your business. You ask, "What goes?" You do, Charlie! Wilma.

WILMA. I have a bad cough and a pain in my lower back which is getting worse and which my doctor says is definitely caused by the separation. This is nothing I anticipated when we got into our difficulties. I'm willing to forgive and forget if you are. Please let me know promptly. I can't even bend down to tie my shoelaces. Charlie.

WILMA. Wherever you are, please listen. Those terrible stories you heard about Singapore and Hoboken can be explained. You belong here with me in New Zealand. My mother agrees. Mortimer.

CHARLIE AND WILMA. If you are listening, *please* get back together! We can't stand the separation. SR/W Box OT.

CHARLIE. You were right. I'm stranded here in New Zealand. The gentleman turned out to be a monster. I know it is asking a great deal but take me back. Please. I love you. Wilma.

NOTICE. We are pleased to report that complete reconciliation has been effected. Charlie has joined Wilma in New Zealand and has a job as assistant professor in American Civilization. Wilma is involved in social work. Greetings to all our SR friends. Charlie and Wilma.

FRIENDS OF CHARLIE AND WILMA. We are planning a little party in New York to celebrate their reunion.

You are cordially invited. Each guest will be required to give short reminiscences of our beloved couple, now happily united in New Zealand. Write for details. SR/W Box US.

WE UNDERSTAND A PARTY is being arranged without us in our honor in New York and that each guest is expected to supply a reminiscence. We will unhesitatingly sue anyone who tells the compost heap story about Wilma the night of the senior prom. Love to all from New Zealand. Charlie and Wilma.

The following is, as far as I know, the only literary analysis of Charlie and Wilma's story.

Article by John Keasler of the *Miami News*

THE SAD SAGA OF WILMA AND CHARLIE

This is the classified saga of Charlie and Wilma.

It may be one of the most publicized romances since Romeo and Juliet although, personally, I think both the plot line and the ending are lots better.

Sherry Woods, the *Miami News* TV and radio editor, was one of many readers of the classified section of the magazine *Saturday Review/World* who got caught up in this story—which appeared a brief paragraph at a time over a period of many weeks.

Unlike most readers she spotted the unfolding story and began to save the notices . . . except for the first couple (who would know that it would go on and on?).

At any rate, the first couple of classifieds ran at widely spaced intervals. Sherry first noticed a warning to a "Wilma" signed by a "Charlie."

Charlie warned Wilma that he knew for a fact that the New Zealander had a wife and two kids.

Now, if you're a "Personals" reader you need no explanation of the interest involved here. We who read personal classifieds can evolve entire novels—nay, entire trilogies—out of a damn sight less than Charlie warning Wilma that he knows for a fact that the New Zealander has a wife and two kids.

Nevertheless, how would Sherry Woods know the story was to continue? None of us—however steeped in love or a good "personal"—could know.

Reading personals is like making a winning pass with the dice—you keep thinking each winning roll is your last. But, by the third personal, Sherry started clipping.

This ran in October 1974:

> WILMA. I don't want you to go off with that New Zealander but if you insist on going through with it, the least you can do is return my baby pictures and cardigan sweater. Charlie.

Charlie, obviously, is a fighter. First, he said the New Zealander had a wife and kids. (It was Hegel who said the most heinous crime is the subtle implantation of doubt. It is also often the most effective measure, in love and/or war.)

Now Charlie reminds Wilma of . . . what memories? His baby pictures! And the cardigan sweater! Ah yes; moments to remember . . . the time we tore the goalpost down, etc.

By November 5, Wilma had come around to answering thusly:

> CHARLIE: Silly boy. "Harry" was just my old uncle, now deceased. I'm still going through with my plans for New Zealand. Wilma.

Hm.

We now have, already, the definite feeling that Charlie and Wilma were made for each other (for better or for worse). Somehow, in the master plan of things, an angle-shooter who asks for his baby pictures back is meant for a lass who uses the old it-was-just-my-Uncle-Harry gambit. . . .

Now we take you to the Personal page of November 30, 1974:

> WILMA. Wherever you are, please listen. Those terrible stories you heard about

154

Singapore and Hoboken
can be explained. You be-
long here with me in New
Zealand. My mother
agrees. Mortimer.

Aha! Can you not see the villain twirling his black
mustache tips? Skulking about Auckland in an opera
cape?

And yet, poor impressionable Wilma obviously had
succumbed to his wiles and his transparent alibis about
Hoboken and Singapore. But who does she turn to in time
of stress? Good old Charlie!

This came on December 14:

CHARLIE. You were right.
I'm stranded here in New
Zealand. The gentleman
turned out to be a mon-
ster. I know it is asking a
great deal but take me
back. Please. I love you.
Wilma.

Then, silence. And then, from an *SR* reader:

CHARLIE AND WILMA. If you
are listening, please get
back together! We can't
stand the separation.
SR/W Box OT.

Finally, early this January, this appeared:

> NOTICE. We are pleased to
> report that complete rec-
> onciliation has been ef-
> fected. Charlie has joined
> Wilma in New Zealand and
> has a job as assistant pro-
> fessor in American Civili-
> zation. Wilma is involved
> in social work. Greetings to
> all our *SR* friends. Charlie
> and Wilma.

If I were Mortimer I would run an ad asking for my
baby pictures back.

Classified Advertising—Personals

Dear Editor:

Your Charlie–Wilma inserts have always intrigued
us—we have been Charlie and Wilma since 1942 (married
thirty-three years).

We surely have been curious about the item.

We have never traveled to New York or New Zealand
but did just return from Kansas City after visiting
Charlie's mom and eating Mother's Day dinner with
her.

Is there really another Charlie and Wilma?

Sincerely,
Charlie and Wilma McKerlie
San Diego, Calif.

Dear Mr. and Mrs. McKerlie:

Mr. K. Jason Sitewell brought Charlie and Wilma into our pages. We assume they are at least as real as sundry other characters he has introduced to our readers. He will be enchanted, I am sure, to know that you are alive and well and living in the fabled land of Southern California.

Thank you for writing.

Sincerely,
N.C.

EDITOR'S NOTE: In answer to requests about details of Charlie and Wilma's party, the *Saturday Review* sent the following response:

Dear Sir or Madam:

We're delighted to hear from you.

The party will be held at 8:10 P.M., Monday, April 21, 1975, at the Essex House, 160 Central Park South, New York City—Room 901. Mr. Cousins will be host. Refreshments will be served.

Each guest will be expected to give a hitherto unknown vignette in the life of Wilma and Charlie (maximum five minutes). Slides will be welcome.

Please let us know if you plan to attend.

Cordially,

Wilma and Charlie Dept. SR

One of the readers, who lived in Boulder, Colorado, had considered making the trip to New York for the party for Wilma and Charlie but wondered whether the party, like most things connected to K. Jason, was real.

Dear Hope Blake:

Warm thanks for your letter. It was much enjoyed, as were the pictures, which evoked all sorts of pleasant memories of my own visit to Boulder and other Colorado haunts. The party was real enough. Some sixty people crowded into the apartment. It was astounding to see how quickly our common interest in Wilma and Charlie made us good friends. Charlie and Wilma were fictional but there was nothing more genuine than the warmth we all felt for one another.

The only disturbing note of the evening came when Charlie's family doctor broke a secret he had kept for more than thirty years. It seems that there was a mix-up in the hospital after the baby was born. The real Charlie, a highly intelligent baby, mistakenly was sent home with the wrong parents. The other baby (who grew up as Charlie) was slightly retarded. The family doctor, who took full responsibility for allowing the double mistake to stand, justified himself by saying that the parents who got the bright baby were so delighted that he didn't have the heart to take the child away, while the parents of Charlie had already made the adjustment. This explains, of course, some of the rather strange classified notices written by Charlie, just as it takes the sting for us out of Wilma's original decision to go off with the gentleman from New Zealand (Mortimer). Perhaps we might give a party for him next year.

Every good wish,
Norman Cousins

158